AFRICAN LEGENDS
OF FAITH SERIES
Volume 2

Enoch Adeboye

Father of Nations

by
❦ Rebecca Bible-Davids ❦

BIBLOS
PUBLISHERS

BIBLOS PUBLISHERS
London, Johannesburg, North Carolina

Published by : BIBLOS PUBLISHERS
4112A North Tryon Street
Charlotte, NC 28206
biblospublishers@yahoo.com

Enoch Adeboye (Father Of Nations)
African Legends of Faith (Vol. 2)
www.alofseries.com
alofseries@yahoo.com
Copyright © 2009 by Rebecca Bible-Davids
ISBN : 978-978-903-541-0

To the beloved memory of
Beatrice Bible-Davids
You left your footprints on the tablet of my heart!

❧ CONTENTS ❧

☀ THE ALOF VISION ☀

With the rolling of the cycle of time, history emerges. However, to the Church of God on earth, history is more than just scientific investigation and the methodical description of its temporal development as defined by scholars. In literal terms, it is actually 'His Story', the story of Jesus Christ and His Church. Unlike any other religion, the Christian faith is deeply rooted in history. Central to the Christian faith is the fact that God came to earth as a man – Jesus Christ. He lived, loved and taught among humanity about 2000 years ago. The historical reality of His sacrifice, burial and resurrection is the keystone of the Christian faith. The Bible is not a fairytale, but a divinely inspired historical record of God's plan of redemption for a hurting world. To study Church history and to take account of today's event which will eventually culminate as tomorrow's history is to see the hand of God at work amidst the transgression of man's ways. The Book of Acts of Apostles which is the genesis of the historical account of the New Testament Church has not reached its conclusions. At every point in Church history, God has continued to raise up mighty vessels, apostles and generals who have continued to champion great revivals.

The historicity of the Universal Church has continued to badly misrepresent, under-represent or simply ignore the actual size of affairs in Africa. The continent has been blurred into margins featuring elaborately ugly pictures of prevailing myths and savage demonic forces forgetting that it is geographically huge, culturally complex and linguistically diverse. However, the history of early and modern Christianity cannot be complete without the mention of the cardinal role played by Africa and Africans. It was prophesied by Isaiah in 750 B.C. (Is. 19:19) and fulfilled by the flight of Jesus' family into Egypt to escape King Herod's tyranny, where the Holy Family eventually found refuge among the Africans. In this seemingly Dark

Continent, the beacon of God's Word has always shone; Africa has been at the centre of God's eternal plan of salvation for all mankind. Right from medieval history of the Church, the people of Africa has continued to be relevant.

In March 2001, I was in Oral Roberts University, Tulsa, Oklahoma, USA and was doing a research on the history of revival movements. I needed to make references to the great revivals across the world. I found vast number of materials and references on Europe and North America, but nothing on Africa. Then, I became even more aware of the missing gap of the lack of documentation of the move of God in Africa in contemporary Church History. Then, the Lord dropped into my spirit the vision to document the works of great revivals and revivalists on the continent of Africa. This birthed the Christian Research Initiative called African Legends of Faith. It is an initiative which works on the International Historic Documentation of African Christian Revivals and Revivalists. The research and documentation are carried out in series looking at the lives and works of African Legends of Faith, one at a time in different volumes.

Since inception, the vision has moved steadily forward. The first volume has been researched and published on the life of the late Archbishop Benson Andrew Idahosa. The research covers the life and works of this great revivalist from an International spectrum. The volume one was indeed an enduring but very successful and fulfilling task. Upon the successful completion of the first volume of the ALOF, the entire board and facilitators by the leading of the Holy Spirit unanimously agreed to embark on the second volume on the person, work, ministry philosophy and faith of the General Overseer of the Redeemed Christian Church of God; Pastor Enoch Adejare Adeboye.

The choice of Pastor Adeboye as a research phenomenon by the African Legends of Faith is based upon the indelible reality of the historic move of the Holy Spirit which has translated into laudable and exceptional feats around the world and massive events which attracting millions of worshippers in one service regularly. Observers have noted it as the first of its kind in the history of Christianity anywhere in the world. Also, it has been observed that the Redeemed Christian Church of God is the world's fastest growing Christian denomination under the leadership of Pastor Adeboye to the glory of God. The African Legends of Faith Initiative believes that all these mighty move of the Spirit of God are worthy of proper research and documentation.

It is our prayers that this work will inspire you towards fulfilling your destiny.

Shalom.

Rebecca Bible-Davids

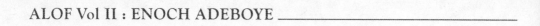

Chapter
1

A Tender Plant In The Desert

The circumstances surrounding the beginning of a man's life does not necessarily determine the end of his life. The mystery of God's infinite wisdom establishes that mostly, he uses the foolish things of the world to confound the wise and the weak to confound the strong.

There is no coincidence in destiny. This striking truth attests to the fact that no child born under any circumstance is a mistake. It doesn't matter whether the child was planned or unplanned, expected or unexpected. After Enoch's parents thought they were done having kids, God imposed his plan and brought about the destiny child that would leave the indelible prints on his generation and forthcoming.

This chapter explains the sovereignty of God that supernaturally nurtured and carefully cherished this tender plant even in the devastating and unpleasant fallow ground of the desert. Rise up friend, your life, marriage, home, business and ministry can also grow like the tender plant in the desert.

Chapter

1

*A Tender Plant
In The Desert*

There is no force on earth greater than when mortal destinies fulfil eternal purposes. The destiny of Enoch Adeboye did not start on the day he was born, it had been conceived in the mind of God in eternity. Heaven kissed the earth on that beautiful morning, when a legend of Faith was wrapped up in disguise and thrown to a poor polygamous family faraway from civilization in a little village called Ifewara.

MOSES THE FARMER

The emergence of a Legend of Faith is usually accompanied with some pivotal moments. The story of this great apostle, Enoch Adeboye cannot be waived aside as it stands as a trailblazer on the rough, rigorous and lonely path that leads to a colourful and glorious destiny. The geographical location and disadvantaged family circumstances surrounding his early life were directly contradictory to the magnanimous future God had reserved for him. This future could only be seen with God's given spiritual inner eyes stacked up with acute spectacles of faith.

Ifewara, Osun State, the tiny village where Enoch Adeboye emerged from is like a speck on the map of Nigeria, West Africa; it is unimaginable how tiny it would be on the map of Africa or on the magnificent map of the world. Prior to the first four decades in the 19th Century, Ifewara had a record of only a few hundred inhabitants.

" If you continue to preach or teach without adequate preparation and prayers, you will only produce half-baked, ill-nourished and spiritually starving flock." - Enoch Adeboye -

Like many other families living in this bucolic village, the family of Moses Adeboye, Enoch Adejare Adeboye's father was not exempted from the struggles and poverty which earmarked their everyday life.

Moses Adeboye, a polygamist had two wives. In those ancient times, Polygamy was the order of the day because it endeared men to having more children, especially male children who would help their parents on the farm work. Like the custom was, the village men married as many wives as they wanted. His first wife bore him six children consisting of three males and three females. On the other hand, his second wife named Esther also bore him four females, out of which one died. At the time, they all lived together in a small house made of mud bricks in Ayesanmi Eyindin Compound, Ifewara.

NO MORE CHILDREN!

Prior to the birth of Enoch Adeboye, his Father Pa Moses already had a large family of two wives and ten children to cater for. He was indeed a hard working man who was much loved by the community because of his good nature but the circumstances of life were not particularly favourable to him; he was really poor. Things were really tough for Pa Moses, his two wives and ten children. They could barely afford one decent meal per day. Moses already had more than enough people to take care of and did not want any more children. However, Esther, his second wife had a different idea. She had bore four girls but did not have any son. In the Yoruba culture where they hail from, a woman was not considered to have a strong ground in her home until she bore a son. So, she was not done with bearing children.

As God would have it, she conceived again. Right from the day she knew that she was pregnant, she began to ask God to make the baby a male child. Esther was a professed Christian, so she trusted in the Lord to make good her request for a male child. She carried that baby in her womb with great hopes for nine months; then came the beautiful sunrise of that glorious Monday morning, the 2nd of March 1942 that ushered in Enoch Adejare Adeboye into the world.

IT'S A BOY!

The day was very exceptional because the entire CMS Churches in Osun State were having a special celebration service in the village. It was towards the noon that labour pains gripped on Esther Adeboye. She began to moan in pains and feel the contractions. When the contractions became too frequent and unbearable, Moses quickly rushed her to a little room in their house where the elderly women and local midwives who had become experts at using local herbs and methods for delivery were called together. In split of minutes, the midwives had surrounded Esther with their wrappers in form of a curtain, while others took delivery of the great legend Enoch Adejare Adeboye.

Pa Moses Adeboye was muttering some words of prayers for his wife who was in serious labour pains as he jangled forth and back outside of their house. Then the cry of a baby broke the silence of perspiration. The midwife shouted, it's a boy! It was indeed a happy day for the couple. The father was happy to have another son who would grow up to be strong and help him on his farm work. The mother was happy that she also had borne a male child who would give her a foothold in her home, but God had other plans. It was not the destiny of Enoch Adejare to be just another egg in the basket. His was the birth of a heavenly messenger, God's anointed. Just as tiny Nazareth played host to the birth of Christ, also the depressing town of Ifewara, is the birth place of Enoch Adeboye.

" You are the determinant of your destiny"
- Enoch Adeboye -

The boy was named Adejare, a name which connotes, 'The Prince who has emerged triumphant or victorious'. Indeed it was a prophetic name because the young Adejare though had a great destiny ahead of him, also had many hurdles to cross and many battles to fight. The first on the list of many challenges that he would face in life was the cruelsome poverty in which he was born. One soothing experience was the fact that the boy was much loved by his mother, and because he was his father's last child who was born to him in his old age, he was also endeared to his favour. Being Esther's last child and only son, she took extra care of him. All he could take was breast milk but it was to an extreme. Even when Adejare began to walk, his mother still continued to breast feed him. As a toddler, he would go and play in the rains with other children but would come back home only to tell his mum he needed to be breastfed. He was so close to his mother's heart and she protected him from any suspecting dangers.

WELCOME TO ABJECT POVERTY

Unlike many who were born into average and comfortable families, Adejare probably went the disadvantaged route. A humble beginning and a happy ending is the best story line. From the moment he set his eyes on the earthly realm, he was welcome into poverty. Everything and everyone around him was poor, he had to grow up as an infant in the very absurd conditions of their tiny mud house which he had to share with close to twelve or more people. They slept almost on each other on the muddy floor. Their standard of living was unthinkable compared to the other poverty ridden people in the village not to talk of comparing it with the luxury of our modern times. They lacked basic amenities.

" Some people want to go to heaven because they believe they will only eat, sleep and loaf around. "

- Enoch Adeboye -

There were no toilets in their village nor in their mud home. The normal procedure for Moses Adeboye, his entire family and the whole villagers was to use the bushes to defecate and use leaves as wipes or tissue. In no time, as soon as Adeboye could walk, he did not have a choice than to go into the bushes whenever he had to defecate. He grew up with other children in their compound as well as his elder ones in the same village.

Soon Adejare was also introduced to going to the streams to bathe and fetch water for the household use. Since there was no electricity in the town, Adejare as a little boy grew in the midst of utter darkness. Their main method of generating light was to walk long distances to the woods, gather firewood and light it up. He grew up to be the favourite of his mum and dad being the baby of the house although it had its disadvantages such as running endless errands for his ten older ones, his father and his mother. When it was time to eat, his mother gave him a special treat such as roasted yam and palm oil, many other times, he would be given (eko ati moimoi) pap with baked beans flour. However, the special treat was not so nutritious but the presentation and love with which he was given made it special.

ADEJARE MY STAR, PLEASE DON'T DIE

Destiny is like a little seed planted by God in the life of a man. At first it was not so obvious to people the kind of greatness that was locked up in this child, God decided to shroud it in mystery. Young Adejare was a very reserved child who was given to much thinking. He was quiet and always inquisitive. Both Moses and Esther were aware that young Adejare was a special child and many signs pointed to it.

As little Adejare grew up by the day, he gained the favour of his parents. And since his parents especially his mother gave him preferential treatments, his siblings were upset and rivalries began. Although the mother of Adejare did not know exactly the enormity of the greatness God had given to him, she knew that he would grow up to be her star and pride.

On one occasion, little Adejare fell terribly ill. At the time, there was no organised health service in the village; they relied solely on traditional healers and spiritualists. He lost his appetite and refused to be fed with any food including his favourite delicacy. His temperature rose very high and his body soon got spotted. The cause of his sickness was as a result of the unhygienic environment they lived in. Regular waste was usually burned or dumped in the backyard of their house and this definitely bred a lot of germs. Adejare was struck with measles, which was life threatening because they had never heard about going to hospital or taking children vaccines.

Adejare's childhood was a bit challenging as he suffered from this unending and persistent measles. Help was constantly sought from different areas in order to treat him and save his life. There was a minute presence of Christianity which was a spill over of the missionary work in that area in the mid eighteenth century, but the people still gave much preference to the worship of different deities and witchcraft activities were prevalent in the village.

When his parents sought traditional help, Adejare would get tempo-rary relief but soon the sickness would come back. On one of such occasions, Adejare became very sick and was rushed to a prophet for prayers but instead of the prophet to pray for his recovery, he began to prophesy. He prophesied that Adejare was a very special child who would grow up to be extremely great. He also said his star was so bright that it would shine and reach the world and make him the father and leader of many Nations. At that instance, that seemed like a rather outrageous prophecy because nobody from the village had seen the lights of the big cities, not to imagine going to different Nations or becoming a leader of Nations.

Moses and Esther looked in amazement at themselves because everyone knew that particular prophet to be very accurate in visions. In their puny minds, they tried to reason out the possibility of the prophecy but if there was any-thing less than nothing, it would be it. It was beyond their calculation, they did not know anyone in Lagos or any big city that could help since they and their friends had not been to a big city. So how on earth would Adejare be a leader when his father was not even able to lead the poorest people in their little village?

" A friend of wisdom is a stranger to foolishness. "

- Enoch Adeboye -

ADEJARE, PICK UP THE CUTLASS

Farming was the major and only source of livelihood for the Ade-boyes'. Ifewara, where they lived was filled with hilly landscape, tropical rain forest and many rivers. These attributes made the land very fertile for farming and this formed the main livelihood of the inhabitants. Since the Yorubas, were vitally farmers; they had a long tradition of passing on the farming heritage to their male children.

Adejare could not be an exception, so they thought.

The family could not wait for Adejare to be up and running on his two feet before they gave him a cutlass and a basket; his farm tools. Grumbling and murmuring began to saturate the family as his older brothers and sisters revolted that Adejare was now able to run and he must be allowed to work. He had to accompany other members of the family to the farm. Although he could not do much being a little boy however his little quota was expected as part of his contribution to the survival of their poverty stricken family.

Pa Moses was always short of resources for his family so they needed to double up their input on the farm work. All hands must be on deck. At the time, farmers had dual residence because the farm was usually a very long distance from home. They combined living in their villages or townships and farm dwellings. So Pa Moses with his older sons could be off to the farm and not return for days or weeks depending on the prevalent circumstances at the farm. There were times they would get there, only to see that bush animals had destroyed some of their plantations. Another factor was the change of seasons. Where they lived was based on seasonal variation of farming needs. When the produce of the farm was harvested, it served as the means of exchange for their other needs.

> " The presence of heavenly walls repels demonic and earthly intruders."
> - Enoch Adeboye -

Not having other options, Adejare was assumed to be destined to follow the same pattern of life of his father and elderly ones. The way of life Adejare saw and lived in was to work hard on the farm, bring home the harvest, eat, sleep, repeat the same routine the next day and that seemed to be his destiny. That was the rhythm in which his life was humanly organised. Growing up in an environment where success was very strange and failure was a norm, it was difficult for young Adejare to dare, to dream, or to talk about visions of greatness.

There was no inspiring role model for him to look up to. Down there, life was very gloomy. He grew up to live in the thickness of ignorance in the air and he felt the very presence of poverty. His father, mother, brothers and sisters were not familiar with greatness in anyway. They were contented with one or two scruffy meals and when it came, they were grateful. Definitely the future was bleak, as they were all unexposed. They lingered in abject ignorance. The scripture rightly says; the poverty of the poor is their ruin. The question I have is how can one hope for what he had never seen or believe what he had never heard? This was the case of the little boy, Adejare, but that is where and when destiny stepped in.

I WILL NEVER TASTE THIS LONG CANE

His father was a disciplinarian who did not give in to sentiments, slothfulness or slackness. Enoch saw this exemplified in the way his father dealt with his siblings when they misbehaved. The strict father, Pa Moses would give rules to the children and no one was bold enough to question him. He had a very long cane he used to chastise anyone who erred. Adejare had an elder brother whom he looked up to and admired. Of course he was little at such a tender age so his brother seemed like a giant to him. One day he was dazed when he saw his father whip the giant brother with the long cane. His brother screamed and cried and Adejare was shocked at the outcome of the spanking, each stroke of the cane left a red long mark on the body of his brother. From that moment, he vowed to do all things possible never to taste the spanking of that long whip.

> " Heaven is not for the lazy but for the hard-working. Saints are gainfully employed in heaven. "
>
> - Enoch Adeboye -

LOST IN THE WOODS

Another significant event happened a few years into his life as a young lad which signalled that he was an exceptional child. His parents and siblings had gone to the farm and Adejare did not know when they left because he had gone out to play some games with his peers. When he returned and asked about their whereabouts, he was told that they had gone out to the farm. In his childishness, Adejare soon set out all by himself to look for them. He had never been to the farm on his own and of course it was a very long and dangerous journey away from home. Even his older siblings were not allowed to go into the woods alone; they had to go in the company of their father.

" Pressure is God's tool for extracting gold from dross. Are you pressurized because of Jesus? Congrats! Your gold is coming out. Total obedience is the most preferred way to revere God."
- Enoch Adeboye -

It was not too long that he got lost in the woods. The place was particularly dangerous and there were reports of how wild animals were rampant in that place and had devoured many people. He cried but nobody was close by. All hope of ever finding the way was lost and he couldn't even find his way back home anymore. Suddenly; a white dog came out of the forest, wagging its tail invitingly and moving in a particular direction. The friendly mien of the dog and the thought that the dog might have come from the farm settlement convinced Enoch to follow it as the dog made its way through forest paths, across tress and fallen timbers.

It was indeed a long walk, but eventually, the white dog led him to the exact location of his parents' farm settlement. When they finally arrived at the settlement, tears of joy flowed from anxious eyes and everyone touched and hugged him in disbelief. When Adejare narrated the story of how he got lost and how the white dog led the way for him, they all marvelled as every one of them were sure that there was no one in the settlement with a white dog. He told them that the dog was around the corner. When they got there, they looked everywhere but they could not find the white dog. They knew that it was a supernatural feat. Since then, his parents knew that he was a special child.

LET'S CALL A PARTY, DAD BOUGHT AN UMBRELLA

If you think that Ifewara was a depressing village with such enormous challenges, the condition of the Adeboye family was even worse. One day, when Moses, Adejare's father was in their compound, many villagers came out pointing to the part of the land where they would build their huts on in the future. The tattered looking people that could barely survive each passing day started pointing to portions of land where their huts would be situated. Suddenly, Moses wanted to join in the league of the wishful thinkers and pointed to a portion of the land claiming that his hut would be built there. To his greatest shock, the group of people shunned him like a little boy, asking him how he could nurse such a lofty idea in his heart as wretched as he was. He felt so discouraged to know that he had now become too poor that even the poor would refer to us as being poor. Theirs was a hopeless condition.

> " One most potent but highly neglected weapon available to every child of God is prayer. "
>
> - Enoch Adeboye -

Few years passed and Pa Moses called his family together. He announced to them that there was a big breakthrough and that it called for serious celebration. With his ego high up like a king, he called all his eleven children and two wives so that he could announce the gigantic reason for the party that was about to begin. It was the miracle of Pa Moses' 'New Umbrella'. Adejare's father had just bought a new umbrella and this was the first time in many years that anything was bought in their house. The women looked for the chubbiest chicken they were rearing; they killed it and threw a party because Adejare's father could finally afford to buy an umbrella.

Chapter

2

*Men Are Born,
Kings Are Made*

Dr. Martin Luther King Jnr once said, "A man who has not found
a reason worth dying for is not worth living."
The little boy Enoch had this intuition and was ready to die for
what he dreamed for against all odds.

Note that the paintings of success are always drawn with the brush
of decision, the ink of determination and on the timeless
plaque of human hearts, if one can dare to dream.

The early life story of Enoch Adeboye revealed in this chapter
vividly paints this picture of possibility against impossibility,
success against failure and progress against retrogression.
Read on and observe how a child of destiny was
tutored and mentored by God Himself!

Chapter

2

*Men Are
Born,
Kings
Are Made*

MY SHOES MUST SHINE TOO!

As a boy, Enoch Adeboye did not have the full picture of the life in the service of God which lay ahead of him. However, in 1951, when he was about 9 years old, something significant happened to him. At that time, the total number of people who had shoes in his village were just five; the school headmaster, the traditional ruler, the catechist, and two others had a pair of shoes each. Only two lorries plied the road to the village in a day, one of which was a Bedford lorry. Even Enoch's father had no shoes, nor his mother and siblings. They all had to walk dangerous paths, tread on hard rocks and sometimes thorns barefooted.

Then one day, it was announced to the entire village that the Archbishop would be paying a courtesy visit to the village. The entire community prepared rigorously to welcome him. It was like the village was expecting God in person as everyone ran helter skelter. Elderly men and women, kids, hunters, farmers, traders, market women; everyone lined up the road on both sides to welcome him. After several hours of waiting with much jubilation and clamour, the hour finally came and there was the man everyone had been waiting for. The Archbishop came in a brand new car which was so attractive. Before that day, Enoch had never seen a car before.

Wow! Enoch was dazzled when he saw the Archbishop step out of his car. He noticed his pair of shoes were shinning and his robe was very clean, sleek and attractive. Simply put, his appearance to Enoch looked so stunning and it was the first of what he had ever seen in life. Again, destiny sprung up in him and he decided that one day, he would be given such honourable treatment, he would wear shinny shoes and be dressed in stunning apparel. When little Enoch got home, he narrated the scene to his mother who also got carried away with his descriptions. Soon, he told his mother that when he grows up, he would become a Bishop too and have a pair of shinny shoes.

Many saw the Archbishop on that day but they could not even dare to dream like Enoch did. It does not matter how impossible a situation looks to you, how high a feat seems impossible to accomplish, all you need is to dare to dream. Though it took well over thirty years of walking up and down in different spheres of life, Enoch Adeboye later became the General Overseer of the Redeemed Christian Church of God. In 1981, he decided to pay a courtesy visit to the parish of the Church in his village. The village got the news of his visit and prepared to welcome him. As it was on the occasion of the Archbishop's visit, the kids, hunters, women and everyone lined up on both sides of the road to welcome him. He also drove to the village in a brand new car, he was wearing a sleek wear and when he came out of his car, he realized he was wearing a pair of shinny shoes. Then he remembered his dream of becoming a Bishop in 1951 which was thirty years earlier. The seed of God does not die.

I MUST BE CELEBRATED

There is no coincidence in Destiny. All of the details of a man's life would eventually form together to form an ultimate whole, which is God's grand plan for man. At the time when Enoch was supposed to start schooling, the Anglican Church started a Primary School; St. Stephen Anglican Primary School in Ifewara village. The timing was so perfect. This was indeed the handwriting of God on the wall. When the local school teacher who was posted to the village arrived, he was welcomed with loud ovation, by the entire village.

The village hunters were making rounds of gunshots. They beat the drum so loudly and danced round in circles and accorded the teacher an honour only worthy of a king. The sight of this was the first inspiration that sparked the desire to be able to stand out of the crowd in Enoch. The urge for greatness, glory and honour sprung up within the young boy. He made up his mind to get to the top at all cost. This was the answer to the questions that had bothered him

> " Not all losses are to be regretted. In fact, certain losses are a blessing in disguise as they will ultimately bring about joy to their victim "
>
> - Enoch Adeboye -

for long, he wanted the better life. He thought to himself that if the school teacher was so much celebrated because he was educated, then he also would love to be educated, so that someday, he would also be celebrated in that manner. Also, the other children were there celebrating the local teacher but only few saw a bigger picture that they could also be celebrated if they chose to. Esther his mother who always wanted the best for Enoch was in full support of his dreams of becoming educated. However, it would not be as easy as said; there was the enormous financial problem of paying his tuition and other expenses.

SEND ME TO SCHOOL OR I DIE!

The family was languishing in poverty and could hardly afford to even feed well. It was an unrealistic ambition to even think of the possibility of starting school in his lifetime not to imagine attempting to go to school immediately. Where on earth will the school fees come from? Although, it was a missionary school and that made it highly subsidised. However, their poor family could not afford his first tuition. The school fees was going to add to their financial burden which was already too heavy. Nobody in his family had ever gone to school, so they did not know the actual advantage of education. It was not going to be an easy task to convince his father to look for the money from impossible sources to pay for Enoch's school fees. But the poor woman decided to give it a trial.

> " Revelation is not an end but a means to an end. Any revelation you receive without running with it becomes useless. "
>
> - Enoch Adeboye -

On many occasions she had wanted to tell her husband of Adejare's decision to go to school but she did not have the courage because she knew she would be asking for an impossible task from him. She got worried about it and tried to look for the best approach to present such request. On a particular day, she noticed her husband was in a good mood so she summoned up courage to make the request. She first began to beat about the bush, trying to set the mood right for this very difficult request, then she began to eulogise his family praises. The moment she made mention of Enoch's intention to go to school, the man who had been attentive, enjoying the praises she had been singing suddenly outraged in anger and disapproval. The request made it look like Esther was inconsiderate and insensitive to their financial circumstances. Pa Moses also wanted the best for his dear son, but the means were obviously not just there. She began to plead with her husband but all her sentiments did not work. After her series of pleading and praising she vouched never to give up on the issue but would find a way to make this dream become a reality.

When Enoch noticed that all his mother's efforts to convince his father to finance his education was futile, he decided to take his destiny in his own hands, so he went on hunger strike. He started to sulk telling his parents there was no point eating when he knew his destiny was about to slip off his hands. He refused any temporary gratification, all he saw was a glorious future and colourful destiny if he could get a chance to be educated like the village school teacher who came to their village. Despite all pleas; he refused to eat any food for the first day, his mother got worried and promised him there would be a way because she did not want him to starve to death.

The second day came and Pa Moses was told that Adejare was going to starve to death if he did not agree to let him go to school. His father thought it was a joke, he yelled and then later pleaded, it was all to no avail. They were all surprised that this young boy was so desperate to change the story of his life. The third day came and the starvation continued. At that point, everyone got scared because he could hardly walk, he was so weak. He continued for that day, but when his father realised that if he did not allow him to go to school, he was desperate enough to die of hunger, so he reluctantly agreed to let him go to school. It was after these three days of hunger strike that the issue of his education was sorted out, although not finally but for a start at least. He was ready to take each day at a time because if he had considered the payment for his total studies, he

> " Giving is the road to the city of wealth. Sacrifice is the key to its strong room. "
> - Enoch Adeboye -

would never start.

It was easy for Enoch to give in to the realities of his impoverished background and not press harder for the privilege to be educated, but he refused to bend his knees to the oppositions around him. He was armed with the determination not to end up like everybody else in the village; he desired to be different and make a difference. His triumph over the opposition of receiving primary education was the first among many triumphs that he would experience in life. If Enoch had given in to the pressures around him and forfeited his dreams of going to school, he might never fulfil the great destiny which God had ordained for him.

A whole lot of people have missed out on their prophetic destiny because they allowed themselves to be intimidated by the oppositions of life. Greatness is for champions and victory is for winners and no one can emerge a winner without a battle. You might be presently faced with a huge mountain that is threatening to swallow up your dreams and terminate your destiny.

" Yes, people are quietly reading your actions, steps, utterances and working at determining the hidden motives as well as who you really are. "
- Enoch Adeboye -

Be encouraged by this assurance that if against all odds, young Enoch Adejare Adeboye overcame the scourge of abject poverty to get educated, you too can overcome. You will overcome.

YEARS OF SACRIFICE

The approval little Enoch had secured with his three days hunger strike from his father was not the solution to the problem of his school fees. In fact it posed a bigger problem because in the actual sense the old man did not have the means to pay for the fees. All hands had to be on deck; sacrifices would have to be made by different people. Enoch's primary education was largely sponsored by a lot of people. There were days when all the proceeds from the hard work of his father on the farm, which should have been used for feeding was used to pay Enoch's school fees. Although, there was so much strain on the family but God met their needs miraculously on many occasions. His mother had to take loans from people; she would run helter skelter seeking for support from friends, foes and family. When the little donations were gathered, it still would look impossible to continue school because it did not cover half of the fees but Enoch was encouraged to press on. Sometimes he would be told not to come to school again because he had not paid, instead of staying home weeping, he would try again. He would go to school pretending everything was alright. When asked by the teacher what was happening, he would give countless excuses and flimsy promises.

All year round, he kept going to school with or without school fees paid. There was a particular time that his schooling was so threatened. Their family poverty seemed to double by the day and continuing his education looked obviously impossible. His mother had taken previous loans from the CMS women fellowship where she had joined, she had exhausted all resources. They were not willing to give her any more loans since she had not paid the previous debts. Just at the verge of giving up, Pa Moses remembered he had his last investment which was his only goat and he had been rearing it for a long time. He did not have a choice than to put the goat out for sale. It was when he did, that Enoch could continue his education. His elder sister Grace was also a huge support to him in elementary education as she continually encouraged him not to give up his dream and that there will always be a way. When classes began again, young Enoch was so excited that he was among the lucky few to have the privilege of education in Ifewara village.

ENOCH, AN 'A' GRADE STUDENT

As school work progressed, Enoch Adeboye began to demonstrate exceptional abilities in his studies particularly in Arithmetic. What he lacked in financial aid, he was able to make up for in academic excellence. Throughout school years, Enoch Adejare Adeboye stood shoulder high above all his colleagues. He was always an A rated student.

It is so amazing how a boy from such a humble background could be that brilliant. That's the mystery of divine destiny. God often hides greatness in seemingly ignoble vessels so that when He manifests His ultimate purpose, all the glory would belong to Him. Right from the cradle through his adult years, there was a great Personality deciphering the hard puzzles of Enoch's life, and that is no other Person but God.

From his Primary School days, Enoch was reported to have been quiet, gentle, humble, obedient and very studious. At the age of eight, he was already the secretary of the Anglican Women Fellowship in Ifewara. He was his mother's joy and his father's pride. He was the first in his family to attend school and the brightest student in the whole school. Little Enoch did not put the investment of the family to waste. He made every tiny cent worth it. So, the family was more encouraged to send him to Secondary School when he completed his Primary School Education.

MY MOTHER, MY FIRST PROPHET

As it became evident that Enoch Adeboye was a child who was very brilliant, hopes began to come alive about the possibility of a bright future for him, away from the limitation of living the rural life and inheriting the family occupation of farming. His mother was his greatest source of encouragement and support. She always pronounced over him pleasant words of blessings. He was made to believe that he was going to be different from everyone else in the village. She saw a brighter future for him and convinced him that he might be born poor, but he could choose to live a life of comfort. He had a strict Christian upbringing which was engineered by a Church going culture, a prevalent style of Christianity of those days.

> " Some Christians argue that they regularly spend time studying the word yet hardly access God's wisdom. The problem may be with their attitude." - Enoch Adeboye -

This Church-going attitude gave him an appreciation of God, but made no extraordinary or outstanding Christian out of him. He would go to the Anglican Church that was close to them with his mother, he continued till he was baptised and confirmed a Communicant (allowed to partake in the communion).

One day after Adejare returned from school and was busy with his books; his mother was so moved by his earnestness. She was not so highly spiritual but God used her tremendously when she prayed and prophesied over him. On a particular day he had just returned from a tedious time in school when his mother began to prophesy on him. She said many prophetic words on him from the depth of her heart, she began to pray that he would be the head and not the tail, she said that when he calls for a person that a thousand people would respond. That last prayer stuck in his heart, he believed it and was highly convinced that it would happen one day. It was indeed a prophetic proclamation; its fulfilment is evident for all to see. No one could have imagined the grandeur splendour of the status where the grace of God would bring him to. Mundane minds could not have imagined that he was destined to become a man of God whom presidents, kings and leaders of nations would come to reverence.

CONGRATULATIONS! LET'S GO BACK TO THE FARM

After Enoch completed his primary education, he came out in fly-ing colours. Everyone celebrated him but thought that at last, there would be some relief from the financial burden Enoch had put on them. They thought his wishful thinking was finally over and that he would return back to work with his family and friends in the farm on a more permanent basis.

Besides he was so lucky that the Primary School started in their village the very year he was to start school. This time, there seemed to be no possible way of going to Secondary School because there was no Secondary School in his village and none was going to start anytime soon. He had no option but to definitely return to full time farm work even now when it was getting close to the harvest season.

However, Enoch had thought far ahead, he was resolute not to end his education on that level. Being a Primary School Graduate made him a star in his family and village but he looked beyond that. At least, he was now more learned than his ten older siblings, he could speak the white man's language in his limited way. At many instances, he would speak an elementary word of English that put his entire family on their toes, clapping for him. He was now a local champion in his family. The level he had reached was good enough in the eyes of everyone in his vicinity.

When he thought deeply on the congratulatory words he received, he decided not to be moved by such praise. For him, it was a time to move to the next level. It was a sign that if he could forge ahead and finish his primary school despite all odds, then it could happen again. He made plans that he would not stop until he had reached a point he could earn some meagre money. He chose to continue till he attained to the level where he could become a Grade Three Teacher so that he could earn some more money to ease the financial burdens of his languishing siblings and struggling parents.

ENOCH GOES TO SECONDARY SCHOOL

Enoch was bent on continuing to Secondary School and would go to any length to get there. There was no Secondary School in Ifewara, the closest Secondary School to his village was so far away in Ilesha. He had no choice, so he decided to travel to Ilesha which is about forty-five minutes drive away. In 1956, he gained admission to Ilesha Grammar School. His total school fee was eleven pounds. That was the first time he would travel out of Ifewara village and it was his very first giant step that would later take him to places he could never have imagined.

The school had boarding facilities which meant that he would be away from home whenever the school was in session. He only returned to Ifewara during holidays. It was a very tearful experience for his family, especially for his mother when Enoch had to leave home for the first time for his Secondary Education. Many of his mates had dropped off along the way because they were contented with the elementary level. So when Adeboye decided to move on, he was forging ahead to becoming a light for his family and the entire community. What they did not realise was that he was a torch-bearer for God and that millions of lives would be illuminated by the light of the torch which he carried.

Life in the Secondary School was very challenging for little Adeboye because he lacked the basic things of life which other students had in abundance. Poverty still had a firm grip on his family, so he could not enjoy the affluence of other kids who had come from the more comfortable families. Enoch Adeboye never wore shoes on his feet until he was 18 years. It was not as though his culture forbade wearing of shoes, but there were no shoes to wear; his parents could not afford it.

In all these tribulations, Enoch Adeboye kept his head up and committed himself to his studies. He knew that education was his only escape away from the degrading life in Ifewara. He was prepared to give life his hardest shots. Enoch was resolute to succeed, by any means necessary. From the hardness which he endured in his childhood years, he learnt to be disciplined and not to take the opportunities of life for granted.

He learnt to value time and he developed a keen sense of punctuality which later became very helpful for him in life. Enoch Adeboye grew up to detest laziness with a passion because hard work coupled with the grace of God was what brought him out of the miry clay of poverty into a life of prosperity and abundance.

YOU CAN ALWAYS DO BETTER

He loved his books with a passion, they were his daily companions. He carried it everywhere he had the opportunity to refer to it. When he returned from school, people teased him about the weight of the bag asking if he was bringing expensive valuables from the white man's land. When other children went out at moonlight to listen to stories, Adejare would go but would immediately return to his books when he got home.

" The one who would succeed and reach his God-given destiny must learn to handle his heart in accordance with divine dictates. "
- Enoch Adeboye -

In Ilesha Grammar school, a particular teacher was never satisfied with the results of the tests he gave them in class. He always inspired the pupils in his class to always do better. However, there were four of the kids that were leading the class in Mathematics and Enoch happened to be one of them.

They always sat together and worked difficult equations out until they got it. Whenever the pupils were given a test on Mathematics, they got high scores like 90%. When they got excited and showed the teacher their score, he would give them an indifferent look and tell them they could do better. The pupils went back unhappy and studied harder. The next test, they scored 95%, this time they sure had done better but their teacher was still unmoved. In great disappointment, the pupils went back and studied night and day working all possible Mathematical problems. The test day came and then they got the dumbfounding score of 100%. They thought the teacher would have no choice as they ran to show him their 100% score. To their greatest shock, the teacher gave them a disdained look and told them to wipe out the grin on their faces because they were rejoicing over 100% score in Elementary Mathematics when their age mates were already in the University. With heads bowed, the kids walked away with a lesson that no matter how good you think you are in anything, there is still a chance to do better.

BORN TO LEAD

Dr Martin Luther King Jnr said, "the true measure of the stature of a great man is not whether he stands in times of comfort and convenience but in those moments of conflict and controversy". Enoch Adeboye stood against all odds, he kept pressing on as a barefooted prince to stop the generational trend of poverty which he was to inherit. He decided that he would be the line of demarcation between the poverty of the past and the prosperity of the future, and that was exactly what happened to him. He made the difference.
While in Secondary School, Adeboye always brought home an excellent result. He endeared himself to the favours of his teachers. His special area of ability was in Mathematics. It was as though his brain

was branded to solve Mathematical equations. No matter how hard the equation was, Adeboye was up to it. He used to take extra hours at solving equations from the textbooks which the teacher was yet to teach the class; so by the time the class opened up on the subject he was already familiar with it. Enoch was always ahead of the class, sometimes by two or three topics. Later in life, Enoch would have to cope with a life of very heavy schedules; however, the Lord had used the rigorous lifestyle of his younger days to prepare him for the greater tasks ahead.

If you know a path without any difficulties, it probably leads to nowhere, the path to greatness is decorated with thorns and thistles to keep you fit for the laurel. Every one of us will have to contend with our personal giants before we get to our place of destiny. Yours might not particularly be poverty like Enoch Adeboye, but no matter in what colour or shade it comes to you, the truth is, it takes conquest to become a conqueror.

From that point, Enoch Adeboye began to develop his ability to teach people. Many of the other pupils formed the habit of asking him to put them through on the subject of Mathematics in which he was an expert. Sometimes after classes, he would start his own little class and teach other students who were having problems with their Mathematics. All through his life, he had always been a teacher. He first began to teach Mathematics at the Secondary School level and later at the University level until the chariot of destiny caught up with him and now, he teaches the Word of life to millions of people around the world. Blessed be the name of the Lord.

It was in the Secondary School that his leadership ability began to manifest. It was not too long before the school authorities noticed his leadership qualities and began to give him the responsibilities of leading the other students when he got to the senior level. One amazing thing is that despite the fact that Enoch Adeboye did not have all the material benefits which other students enjoyed due to his impoverished background, he never allowed that to intimidate him in any way or to form in him a sense of low self-esteem. The young lad believed in himself to a fault. He had this strong aura of leadership around him. He talked and walked with confidence. A wise man once said, "A man can't ride your back unless it's bent." Enoch refused to bend his back. Just like the Biblical Daniel and his comrades who were carried into slavery but did not allow their circumstances to overshadow their destiny. Similarly, despite his financial limitations, Enoch Adeboye's star shone so brightly among his peers.

ATTRACTIVE BUT ATTENTIVE

In his adolescent years, Enoch grew up to be a very tall, healthy and energetic young man. He grew so tall to about 6'2, broad shouldered, dark skinned. Enoch Adeboye was by all standards, an attractive man. Wherever he went, he stood taller than almost everybody. Enoch is naturally gifted with very deep baritone voice and he is soft spoken; all these added charm to his oration. Later in his life, these qualities have become very useful in ministry. His messages are always like burning coals of fire, but he delivers them in his usual soft and gentle tone that gives it a cushioning effect and keeps listeners spellbound.

He was not very sociable but he had a very close friend by the name, Rotimi Akinseinde. They were two jolly friends and they did almost everything together apart from farming. Enoch enjoyed fishing and catching squirrels. Up till now, he still loves fishing. There was a particular stream in Ifewara where Enoch loved to relax. He was so familiar with the stream that if he was not in the farm you could instantly predict that he would be at the stream catching fish and swimming in its flowing waters. In Secondary School, he was not extremely good in sports but was in the Aranmolaran House (Sports club). The different sport houses used to play competitive games such as 100 yards race, against each other. Adejare excelled in other activities and was extremely quiet and studious.

All through his younger years, Enoch Adeboye was always a lady's man and this started right from the Secondary School days. The girls always flocked around him, but he maintained his cue. Though he had all the qualities to ignite attraction from the opposite sex; he was tall, dark, handsome, and very brilliant. He also had a very soft and charming voice; everything seemed perfect except the monies. He could not afford any distraction. He remembered he had come a long way so he kept his head straight. He was attractive and charismatic but he paid full attention to his studies.

BEES! BEES! BEES!

Whenever the school was on holidays, Enoch would return to Ifewara to help his parents on the farm work and would do other menial jobs in order to save little money to supplement the little which his parents would give him.

Sponsoring his Secondary Education was even more challenging than his Primary Education. He was threatened severally to be sent out of the school. Although he was brilliant, he was not excused from paying his school fees. The poverty increased by the day and pressures began to mount on Enoch ranging from his teachers, to the registrar, to the headmaster, to his parents, and to his siblings. Everything pointed him to only one way which was to be content with his present position and drop out of school.

Every time there was a break in school, it was a mixed feeling of relief and pain. Relief from the pressure of school authorities monitoring him for his fees owed but on the other hand, 'Pain' because he had to go back home in Ifewara, the cradle of poverty and extreme labour. Although he was always welcome home like a star when he returned home but he could not wait to finish school and relieve his family of the rigorous lifestyle they all lived.

When he came home on holidays, he had to go deep into the woods to cut down some logs, to sell and get some money. There was a day when he went into the woods to cut down some logs and then he accidentally got stuck on a bee nest. The bees were enraged and swarmed out in tens and stung him in the face and on the arm. Enoch ran for his dear life and shouted; "Bees! Bees!! I have been stung by bees". Amazingly, he still had the determination to pack the log of wood which he had cut before the bees attacked him. The log of wood was not going to be given up under any circumstance because that was part of what would make up his next session school fees. The young man would not allow anything, not even the excruciating pains from the sting of bees to deprive him of the little pennies that he would get from the sales of the wood. Even in the midst of pain, he was not distracted. He chose to be focused.

> " The world demands wisdom in your life as proof of knowing Christ. Do you have it ? "
> - Enoch Adeboye -

MY SINS ARE IN THE PIT

As they were about leaving Secondary School, Adejare's friend called him aside to make a confession. The boy had been very naughty in school and was bent on turning a new leaf since everyone was leaving school to become something good in life. He confessed that he used to steal the hens which belonged to the teachers living around the school premises; he also sneaked out of the school on many occasions and had many bad adventures outside at night. He would cheat in class while they were having examinations and lie about everything. He knew his truancy would lead him to a bad end so he was ready to make a change.

After all his confessions to Adejare, he pleaded that they should walk far away from the eyes of people, which they did. When they got there, the boy dug a hole very deep in the ground and began to make all those confessions into the hole loudly. He also started making pledges that he would never return to his mischievous ways. Adejare watched him because he did not know at the time the importance or significance of what the boy was doing. But one thing was sure, the boy was ready to make that turn to good.

> " What you say or believe about God does not add or subtract from who He is, except of course in His personal relationship with you. "
> - Enoch Adeboye -

BORROWED OVERSIZE TROUSERS AND SHOES

The five years which Enoch Adeboye spent at Ilesha Grammar School seemed like ten years because his education was very tough. It was threatened at every point to be disrupted because of extreme poverty. Credit must be given to his mother who stood with him as a rock-solid support. Whenever it looked like he had reached the very dead end and might have to drop out of school, she would stick out her neck and go all the way to do some extra work, get a loan from a relative or sell some of her personal belongings. Enoch's Primary and Secondary education was mostly financed by women especially his mother, his sister Grace, and the women at the Anglican Women Fellowship, where Enoch served as a kid secretary.

He continued his studies working excellently to become a source of inspiration to his parents. He was determined to relieve them from the poverty that had gripped them tightly. When he was about to complete his Secondary School as a final year student, there was a sudden news that came to him. His father had died. He was shocked when the principal told him and accompanied him to pay his last respect to his father who had become frigid. After the news, he was upset but could not help the situation so he was returned to school to face his final examinations.

In 1960, at the age of 18, Enoch Adeboye completed his Secondary School Education and came out in flying colours. He had straight As' in all subjects. He became the first person to attend school in his family and one of the very few to attend Secondary School in his place of origin. The fact that he had completed his Secondary School did not automatically put poverty out of his life; he still had a lot of challenging financial situations.

His brilliance and excellence in his studies made him excel so much. Now the Prize Giving Day and Valedictory Celebration were fast approaching. It dawned on Adejare that he did not have any presentable trousers to wear on the day. For shoes? He had never owned or worn one all his life. It was supposed to be a day he would be looking forward to but it was more of a day he dreaded because the shame that he was bound to experience was glaring straight at his face. As the day approached, the tension increased because he could not afford a pair of shoes or trousers at the time. The most dreaded part of his imminent disgrace was that since he was so intelligent, he had to receive most of the prizes of the day. This meant that he was going to be called on stage several times in the presence of all students, staff and parents.

When the day of his valedictory came, God made a way for him as usual, although he still could not afford to buy any wears, he had to lend from his relative who pitied him. It was his first time of wearing a shoe as he posed in the borrowed over sized trousers and shoes on his Celebration day. From that point on, Enoch Adeboye resolved to keep pressing forward until he reached the very pinnacle of his career. If by the grace of God, he could overcome the quandaries of poverty to pass out of the Secondary School in flying colours, it seemed that with more hard work and determination, he could achieve anything. Courage and confidence began to build up in him. He was feeling the aura of possibilities that with God on his side, he could proceed further to the next level of his education.

From the story of Adeboye's childhood, it is clear that the stones that form the very foundation of any man's towering heights of greatness are those indispensable stones of integrity, hard work, endurance, commitment, focus and ruggedness to mention a few. Enoch Adeboye like every seed of greatness took deep roots in the earth before he shot out to become the mighty tree that he is today.

Right from the beginning, Enoch Adeboye has had an insatiable drive for excellence, he never settled for the less. Like Oliver Twist, he always wanted more. He could have settled for the First School Leaving Certificate like many of his peers did, but he pressed forward to Secondary School. After he graduated from the Secondary School in flying colours, he could have stopped; at least that could get him a job as a village Primary School Teacher. Enoch Adeboye wanted more for himself, he aspired for a greater level and because the manifold grace of God was mightily at work in his life, he was able to climb up the ladder under the most stringent conditions of poverty.

Chapter

3

Enoch, The Leading University Actor

Why does the Bible warn young people to
remember their Creator before the evil days come?
Here the life of Enoch Adeboye as an undergraduate depicts
the pitfalls of many young people who get carried away by youthful
exuberance. The enemy is still in the business of creating an
overblown picture for temporary gratification which
often sways innocent young people into the dark
world of infidelity, drunkenness, disobedience,
peer pressure and false fame.
This chapter unfolds the simple event of life that made
this young handsome dude, Enoch Adejare Adeboye
determine to pay back the feminine gender
with unfaithfulness and infidelity.

Enoch, The Leading University Actor

I REFUSE TO DIE A SERVANT

Enoch experienced many sad days after completing his Secondary Education due to the low economic status of his family. He had to go back home into farming in order to help his family. Nothing had changed much in his village except that he now had more knowledge but nowhere to apply it. It seemed like a devastating season where he had left where he was but had not arrived in the place he was going. This time, he couldn't venture telling his mother to sponsor him to University because she had exhausted all her resources. Besides, his father was now deceased leaving all the financial burden of the other children on his poor mother. There was no place to extend his faith anymore because he had finally reached his limits since University Tuition Fees were far more expensive than Secondary School.

In the midst of his dark and hopeless season, it seemed like a spark of light was appearing when a distant relative showed up. The woman promised Enoch's mother heaven and earth that he would sponsor him throughout his University Education. Excitements filled the air as his mother rejoiced thanking God for sending help through the woman. Enoch packed his bag, waved goodbye to farming again and off he went with this woman. The young man was fascinated with the new environment he was brought into and decided to leave a mark. Still full of hopes and expectations about his University Education, he decided to make himself useful to the relative in appreciation. So, he began to help with all the household chores. Soon, his spirit of excellence and diligence singled him out. He was so helpful, honest and obedient that the woman got so impressed and committed more work into his hands. He continued there as weeks went by, then months and months.

When he raised the issue of his school, it was ignored and swept off. Now, it seemed like the lady was beginning to enjoy his free service and was not willing to help. She wanted him to remain there serving her and forget about his aspiration of going to University. She was looking for a house help and she thought God just brought her one. Little did she know that she was hosting a man on a mission! When he realised that he had reached a dead end with the lady after several pleas and persuasions, his mother advised him to return home. He did. Full of regrets because the relative did not keep to her word, he was ready to pick himself up again and would not give up his dream of becoming a University Graduate. The action of the lady angered his mother but she had no alternative for her son. All she had was to speak prophetic words of success and blessings to him by the day. Madam Esther Adeboye being a woman of strong faith believed that God would see him through his University Education miraculously just as He had seen him through his Secondary Education.

GOD'S SPECIAL PROJECT

The University of Nigeria Nsukka, popularly known as UNN was founded in the Eastern Region of Nigeria as the first indigenous

University. The University was formally opened on 7 October 1960, as the climax to the Nigerian Independence Celebrations in the Eastern Region. Her Royal Highness, Princess Alexandra of Kent, representing Her Majesty Queen Elizabeth II at the Nigerian Independence Celebrations performed the opening ceremonies and laid the foundation stone of one of the University's early buildings.

It is noteworthy that the hand of Providence which brought Primary Education to the little village of Ifewara at the perfect time for young Adejare to commence schooling also was at work to open wide the gates of University of Nigeria Nsukka, at

> " The human heart is so depraved and wicked that it takes God's grace to tame it continually. "
>
> - Enoch Adeboye -

about the same time when he passed out of Secondary School and wanted to pursue his University Education. There has always been a consistence in the sequence of events in the life of this great Legend of Faith. It is not by sheer act of coincidence but the mighty hand of God working behind the veil of his life to unravel the mysteries and put the little dots of his life together to make the ultimate whole.

The hand of God for the life of Enoch Adeboye had always been so strong that whenever he got to a crossroad in his life, the doors always swung open before him. Also in his lack, God always made provisions. The desires of his heart were always miraculously granted, even if those things were not there prior to his arrival, his heavenly Father would create them, just for him. Right from the beginning, Enoch Adeboye had been God's project; God's seed that never dies. Prior to his University Education, he continued to contend against that fierce monster called poverty which always threatened his amiable destiny. Though he was one of the most brilliant pupils of his days, he could not proceed into the University immediately because of financial constraints.

I CAN'T STOP HERE, I HAVE NOT ARRIVED!

In between his completion of Secondary Education and admission to University, he had to go and teach briefly in a local school where he was able to keep some little savings for his mother, siblings and his University education. In 1962 he sent in his application and gained admission in 1963 to the renowned University of Nigeria Nsukka for B.Sc in Mathematics. Enoch Adeboye received his admission letter with mixed feelings. He was excited that he was making progress towards the pursuit of his dreams; however, the thoughts of the huge financial constraints saddened his heart. He encouraged himself and determined never to give up on his dreams of breaking the jinx of poverty in his family lineage.

> " You can move from being limited to what your brain can accommodate, to the unlimited level of knowledge that your spirit man by the power of the Holy Ghost can access. "
>
> - Enoch Adeboye -

After working on the farm, selling wood and saving his meagre teaching income, he decided to give his admission a shot. As usual, nothing around him was encouraging but he forged ahead, encouraging himself by the day. At last the day came and with little or nothing, Enoch Adeboye set out on a journey of more than thirteen hours by road from Ifewara his birthplace in Osun, Western Nigeria towards the place where he would be studying for the next four years; University of Nigeria, Nsukka, Enugu, Eastern Nigeria. By the time he completed his University Degree, he would have distinguished himself as a man to be reckoned with.

A University degree would prepare him to face the open world. He would be qualified to get a decent job and have a good life against the backdrop of his poverty stricken background. Moreover, there were not so many University Graduates in Nigeria at that time.

Upon the successful completion of his University Degree, Enoch Adeboye was poised to become one of the few elites in the Country. Unlike many others who made it like himself, the peculiar situation of his impoverished background made his success particularly outstanding.

THE HEAD, NOT THE TAIL

Enoch Adeboye went to the University with one purpose; to study hard and graduate with a first-class. He did not indulge himself in all the vices that other students were busy with. He was a typical bookworm. He took his spare time to solve Mathematical problems. Enoch Adeboye topped the class and the Faculty. He worked hard and calculated himself to a first-class honours student just as he had envisioned. His grade points were very high and he was soon noticed by the lecturers and students.

Being in a new terrain, he was very reserved and quiet. He did not spare any time in waste, he was so desperate to achieve his destiny that he would spend hours and hours locked up solving a particular Mathematical problem that others had given up trying. Avoiding all forms of distractions, he would spend quality time cramming many Mathematical equations and formulas.

FREE MEALS

As soon as Adeboye heard that there was a possibility to receive free meals in school, he was ready to dig out the information to its roots. He had come to University in a strange and unfamiliar territory and all he had was not sufficient to see him through his first semester, not to think of all the years he would be studying, so he knew he would have to grab every opportunity possible. While searching for the authenticity of the information he had just heard about the free meals and other benefits, he realised it had to do with being a sportsman. It was an opportunity for people who wanted to join the University of Nigeria Volleyball Team. He was not really a sports person; he was more of a quiet and studious mathematician. Not minding whether he had special interest in sports or not, he jumped at the offer since he was not sure where his next meal would come from. He had to press on, dropping out of school would mean going back to poverty which to him was not an option.

The qualifications for potential Volleyball Team Members was to be able to run one mile at a stretch, do ten press-up exercises and lift some weight. Adeboye's ears tingled as he heard the benefits that followed. His main interest was not representing the school, playing volleyball, running or doing press-ups. It was the fact that he would get free meals and other fringe benefits. His energy doubled as he woke up very early in the mornings and jumped out to practice running, press-ups and weight lifting. At the time of the test for the choice of team players, Adeboye could not be ignored because he had practiced so well that he could do double of what he was asked to do. He was able to run two miles, do twenty press-ups and lift unimaginable weights.

MY MOST TRUSTED VIRGIN

Adeboye continued in school. He was full of hopes and goals and desperately wanted to liberate his family. He did not want to make the mistakes of his father who had many children and could hardly provide for them. Hence, he chose to be straight head, gentle and studious. Since he was not born again at the time, all his friends were unbelievers.

In the midst of his worldly friends that had fleet of girls at their beck and call, Adeboye being an Anglican had a slight moral judgement of good and bad. So, he looked round his circle and found a nice looking girl who appeared good in terms of beauty and character. He summed up courage and approached this beautiful 'virgin', asking her to be his girl-friend. The girl felt so honoured to be chosen by the tall, dark,

" If God permanently resides in you, you would have become His headquarters. God's headquarters is Satan's none-quarters. "

- Enoch Adeboye -

handsome and intelligent dude called Enoch Adeboye. Enoch was full of hopes on the kind of home he would build; he had already started painting a vivid picture of how both of them would live together as husband and wife with love and honesty. Since he had decided to have just one girlfriend, he stuck to her alone, nurturing and preserving her for their married life to be.

On several occasions, he would be with his friends and would watch how they had many girlfriends at the same time, but would smoothly tell uncountable lies to each of the girls. He watched them defile many gullible girls but he shook his head in disappointment at their behaviour. His friends tried to influence him to cheat on his girlfriend but he was so determined because he loved the girl dearly and had promised her his commitment. At other times, they made fun of him but he stood his ground.

It was like glass thrown against a rock to be shattered when Enoch discovered the unfaithful deeds of his most trusted "virgin". His heart was broken. His planned future bride had been flirting and cheating with other guys while he was so adamant on his commitment to her. It was a big shock to him. He could not believe he had been the victim and fool all the while. This made him take a new turn. He then concluded that his friends were the right match for ladies. From then on, he decided to make a mess of the feminine gender. He would never be fooled again and other ladies would have to pay for the sins of their sister who broke his heart.

THIS MUST BE LIFE

His new school environment was a bit tempting. He suddenly realized he was on his own totally far away from his parents and did not have to be accountable to anyone; all his decisions were made alone for himself and by himself. Then he knew he was becoming a man and must be a responsible one. Reacting to his recent heartbreak he engaged in youthful exuberance although he still kept his mind upright. He did not get carried away nor did he lose his focus, he knew how to balance his life. One thing was so sure; he never wanted to go back to the poverty and wretched environment he came from.

At this time, Adeboye had become a brilliant mathematician and all that filled his head was solving equations and formulas. He had little time for religion. He had the general knowledge of God but He did not have the saving knowledge of Jesus Christ. Not long after, he got familiar with the environment and his colleagues began to clamour round him. His intelligence and leadership traits soon sold him out again and then the ladies began to throw themselves at him when they needed someone to put them through tough Mathematical problems. They came in numbers and tried to distract him. Being young and full of life, he decided to let down his guards especially after he had just been disappointed by the 'one virgin' he trusted.

Although his education did not lack, he began to try what his friends were doing. Before he knew it, being naturally very smart, he had become a professional in drinking choice wines and spirits, flirting with pretty ladies, leading his cliques in parties and being an attractive undergraduate. He began to think life had just begun. This kind of life did not exist where he came from in Ifewara. They were a bunch of ignorant and unexposed people. He began to think everything was under control because all he wanted was within reach. He did not have to starve or beg for anything desperately because the ladies flocked around him and made sure such needs were met. Farming? It had finally become a closed case in his life for good.

ADEBOYE, THE GANG LEADER

As he gradually continued to slide into sin, he realized that he had begun to enjoy sports. As his leadership personality arose, he chose to be the best he could even in sports. He needed the social acceptability to be his gang leader and not just a follower even in sports. Students in his clique were already his followers as they accorded him respect and honour. This meant he had to work harder to keep the members of his gang looking up to him.

He wanted to be well built with muscles so he chose boxing as his love sport. Boxing, not being an easy sport would make anyone fret, however Enoch did not mind the threatening dangers that accompanied his choice. The rationale

" Many people believe that the days of divine visitation are over; but I bring you good news that yours is just beginning. "

- Enoch Adeboye -

behind the decision was that since he could not stand to be bullied, boxing would also come in handy as a means of protection against any harassment that might come his way. It would also instil confidence in his followers that he was capable of protecting them in case of impending dangers. He was extremely good at boxing as he normally defeated his opponents leaving them helpless. He fought and beat rival gangs, not minding the repercussion on his body. However, he emerged the champion and leader of the gang that everyone feared to step on campus and no one dared to bully him and his gang followers.

I CAN'T DIE NOW

During his days at the University, there was so much civil restlessness across Nigeria which later escalated into the Nigerian Civil War between July 6, 1967 and January 15, 1970. The core contention of the war was essentially economic, ethnic, cultural and religious tensions among various peoples of Nigeria. The impact of the war was felt by all and sundry. There was conflict on the few University campuses that were in Nigeria at that time. Students were attacking their colleagues who hail from other parts of the Country. Enoch Adeboye a Westerner, schooling in the Eastern region, had very bitter experiences of the pro-civil war hostility. His best friends from South-Eastern region of Nigeria at the University suddenly became his sworn and vicious enemies. He had to run for his dear life. He crossed the River Niger in a dugout canoe, bailing water from it in the dead of the night.

It was a very bizarre experience for him, but he remembered the words of his mother when he was travelling that he would travel and come back safely. She had also assured her son that they will meet themselves in unity when he needed to return. Memories of his mother's prophecy that he would be lifted in life, so much that when he called one person, a thousand people would respond to him, raced through his mind. He believed every word his mother told him and since a thousand people had not started to respond to him, he knew he couldn't die yet. These were the words and convictions that kept him moving against all odds in the middle of the sea. Many of his colleagues died during this time but God preserved his life. By the supernatural help of God, he received strength to survive the ordeal of crossing the Niger from Asaba to Onitsha with his discovered local canoe.

A GRADUATE AT LAST

After all the ordeals of his financial constraints coupled with the problems of the civil war, in 1967 at the age of 25, Enoch eventually graduated with First Class Honours. One hour of glory can compensate for a lifetime of agony. For Enoch Adeboye, the Convocation Ceremony was very peculiar. It represented his victory over the struggles of impoverished background which had walleyed him right from the cradle. It also represented a lofty reward of meritorious hard work. The Convocation was his gift to his mother who had sacrificed all she had to see him through; to the family that encouraged him right from the beginning and to the community from where he came.

At this juncture, I sense that someone reading the story of this Legend has a pressing need to pull through a difficult season. Also if you need to break a family jinx, tap into the doggedness and resilience exemplified in the life of Enoch Adeboye. It is within your reach only if you extend your faith and do not give up. There is always a way and answer on the other side if you press on. Step out, step up, and move on because you can do it. If Enoch was blessed so much that he changed the history of his family and brought honour to his entire community, your life also can be an exceptional one that will break a family, national, tribal, community, gender or religious record. Don't give up! You can make it!

Chapter

4

Foluke, Will You Marry Me?

Marriage is not a child's play neither is it by trial and error.
If one makes a wrong choice of partner,
he has made a big mistake.
Choosing the right person takes spiritual
sensitivity, prayer and wisdom.
Enoch Adeboye, although unsaved when choosing his bride
Foluke, yet he was able to discern by spiritual calculations the
unique inestimable qualities of the young lady.

If you are single and you feel uneasy about your choice
of an intending life partner, seek counsel, pray and watch
out for the fruits produced by the proposed partner.
The scriptures confirm that 'by their fruits,
you shall know them'.

Chapter

4

*Foluke,
Will You
Marry Me?*

ADEBOYE, THE LADIES MAN

Prior to graduating from the University, the young, tall, dark, handsome and brilliant Mathematics Undergraduate at UNN was the toast of all the young women in town. Everything about him was a huge point of attraction to the ladies. There were not many University students around; he was actually one in a thousand. The girls flocked around him and every one of them wanted to be the number one of the handsome Enoch Adeboye. Whenever he came around for the holidays, he always received many gifts from the ladies who were trying to gain his attention.

In his youthful days, Enoch Adeboye was indeed a ladies' man. He once admitted; "before I met the Lord Jesus Christ, I had some problems. The first one was that I was a sportsman. The second one was that I was a good photographer. Combine those two in the life of any young man and you know he can have problems with girls. I am yet to meet a woman you tell that you want to take her picture and she would refuse. Before you know it, they (the women) are already adjusting their dresses, and from picture taking you move to something else. I had so many girlfriends that I did not even know the number at a stage".

Among all the ladies who befriended Enoch Adeboye was a particular and special one, who stood out and stole his heart. Her name was Foluke Adeyokunnu. She was a slim, dark skinned, small framed and vibrant young teenager. Enoch met Foluke in 1965. Enoch was a friend to one of Foluke's cousin who lived in a city called Ibadan. He normally visited Foluke's cousin's house anytime he was on holiday from University. On the other hand, Foluke was schooling at United Missionary College Ibadan popularly called UMC, a Teachers Training College. Enoch and Foluke met there a couple of times and they soon blended as good friends.

Incidentally, Enoch and Foluke were Science and Mathematics Majors; so they often spent time together, discussing academics and campus life. Because they were both in school, the only time they had to interact was during the holidays. The two began to look forward to their holiday period when they would meet. Their meetings were full of laughters since they waited to share their experiences. Most times, they had a lot to catch up on. However, Enoch who had other girlfriends was not thinking of committing himself to either Foluke or any other person in a serious relationship; it was all supposed to be just a fling but God had better plans concerning the woman who would later become the jewel of his life, Miss. Foluke Adenike Adeyokunnu.

" Earthly wisdom comes by age: divine wisdom comes by the spirit. "
- Enoch Adeboye -

HOSPITABLE FROM BIRTH

Foluke Adeyokunnu was born into the royal family of Papa Jacob Adelusi Adeyokunnu and Madam Felicia Morounfola Adeyokunnu in Ilesha, Osun State of Nigeria, as the first in a family of ten chil-

Pastor Enoch Adeboye speaking
The Word of Life.

Pastor Enoch Adeboye (25) and Pastor Mrs Folu Adeboye (19)
on their wedding day, September 8, 1967.

Pastor Enoch Adeboye shakes hand with Pastor Mrs. Folu Adeboye to congratulate her when she graduated from the Bible College over thirty years ago.

Left to right – Pastor Mrs Folu Adeboye , Pastor Enoch Adeboye, Pa Josiah Akindayomi and Mama Akindayomi on the occasion of Pastor Adeboye's Ph.d (Doctorate)Award convocation.

Pastor Adeboye and Pastor Mrs Folu Adeboye in Sydney, Australia during one of their early foreign missionary trips.

Family picture of the Adeboyes' in 1998.

Pastor Enoch Adeboye interpreting for Pa Akindayomi (service to God and his anointed). Humility and discipline are the keys to upliftment.

Pastor Adeboye eulogise Poetic praise to God in the 2008 Church Convention.

If you think Daddy G. O. cannot play football, think again.

Pastor Enoch Adeboye and Pastor (Mrs.) Folu Adeboye giving thanks to the Lord for the success of one of the Church conventions.

Pastor Enoch Adeboye and Pastor (Mrs.) Folu Adeboye digging it unto the Lord during the dinner night of the Apostles Fellowship Int'l Conference 2009.

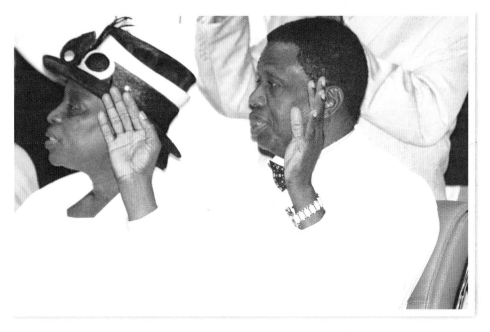

Pastor Enoch Adeboye and Pastor (Mrs.) Folu Adeboye worshipping the Lord at the Church Convention 2008.

Pastor Enoch Adeboye addressing the grandaunts of the Bible College in 2006.

dren on Tuesday, 13th July, 1948. Her father, Pa Jacob Adeyokunnu had a long and successful career as a teacher with the Methodist Mission Nigeria. He was also a very devout Christian. He was in fact the Church's Catechist, which is known today as a Deacon or an Associate Pastor. He imbibed strict Christian values into his children. Being a disciplinarian, he made it compulsory for them to attend Church services.

Foluke's mum was a very industrious woman who traded in clothes and merchandise. She was successful and prosperous and many in the neighbourhood loved her because she was kind and generous. Although their family was a polygamous home with more than a wife, however it was still a habitation of love and peace. Foluke grew up in the midst of love, she never experienced hatred or hostility in her childhood days. Her father always instilled into her the values of self-confidence. He reassured her that she could become whatever she wished. So, young Foluke grew up knowing that everything within the parameters of her destiny was possible.

Because she was the first child in such a large family, she was always laden with the responsibility of taking care of her younger ones; she had to do the cooking and cleaning of the entire household. She was very hard working and had flair for things to be in perfect order. Right from her early days, she developed the ability to cook and cater for very large numbers of people with ease. Unknowingly, God was using all these to prepare her for the responsibility of greater tasks and coordinating the peaceful care for millions of guests later in life. God's processes sometimes seem to contradict his purposes but they are actually working at a distance to accomplish them.

Foluke attended Methodist Primary School, Ilesha and Methodist Girls' Grammar School respectively. She was a very bright student and modelled excellence for all the other children in the neighbourhood. After the successful completion of her Secondary Education, Foluke proceeded to attend the United Missionary College, Ibadan, in Oyo State of Nigeria. She completed her studies in flying colours and graduated as a Grade Two teacher at the age of eighteen.

FOLUKE WAS DIFFERENT

It was during her time at UMC that she met the man with whom, she would share her destiny, the young Undergraduate of Mathematics from the University of Nigeria Nsukka, Enoch Adeboye. Enoch being the popular handsome dude in town, was a socialite and always celebrated his birthdays in special ways. Also his girlfriends would use the occasion to send him special gifts in order to win his heart and endorsement to be his potential wife. On the occasion of his birthday as usual, all his girlfriends were presenting him with all sorts of love gifts, special cards and romantic poems, Foluke was different. Foluke presented him with a small New Testament Bible and two snow white handkerchiefs. Though she did not have a saving knowledge of Jesus Christ, she was well brought up in a Christian home and knew that the Word of God supersedes all things.

That simple act had a great deal of impression on the heart of Enoch. He later admitted "By the time I got these gifts, something in me made it clear to me that this is the woman I will marry." It was not as though Enoch was saved at that time, but he was also raised in a Christian home and knew that a woman, who valued the Word of God above the frivolities of life, would make a good and faithful wife. This act Foluke made, resurrected his earlier desire for chastity which the first lady tore down. He concluded that Foluke was different from the other ladies who cheaply threw themselves at him. He made up his mind to do away with the other girls and get serious with Foluke. Enoch made the right choice.

LOVE BIRDS SAY I DO

Proposing to Foluke was not going to be an easy thing but Enoch was capable of wooing any lady with both his looks and charisma. Foluke was known to be very decent, blunt and plain. She was the kind of person that would call a spade a spade. She could not tolerate liars and deceivers and was ready to correct and rebuke one that she met. She had the special combination of pleasantness and firmness. So, Enoch was careful not to receive a negative answer from her, since he had not got one from any lady. He put himself together, full of charm and optimism, he followed his heart and went ahead to propose marriage to the woman of his dreams.

Foluke also had some suitors who were interested in her, however, she knew what she wanted from life and she gave Enoch a 'yes'. She later said, what attracted her to Enoch was the fact that he was very real and simple. While the other men were busy promising heaven and earth, Enoch never promised what he could not do, and he always lived up to his words. In those days, a girl could not make a singular decision to marry a man. It was the duty of the bride's family to make sure the groom was from a responsible background. Though Foluke had fallen over her heels

> " Failure comes when spiritual tasks are essentially carried out by physical strength. "
> - Enoch Adeboye -

for Enoch, the major decision lied with her father, Pa Jacob Adeyokunnu. So, Foluke found a way to pass the message to her father and to her greatest delight, he asked to meet Enoch and he liked him. As God would have it, the old man gave his approval and the two lovebirds began their journey of love into a future filled with many adventures of life.

At that time Enoch was twenty-five and Foluke was nineteen. They had a brief but interesting Courtship. Pa Jacob Adeyokunnu being the disciplinarian and also a minister with the Methodist Church kept a close watch on their relationship. He made strict rules for them. Enoch could only visit his daughter if someone else was present. If they went for a stroll, it had to be for a very short time.

> " When you engage in consistent, intense, and the soul touching type of prayer, power is released to enable you overcome life's challenges. "
> - Enoch Adeboye -

Those years, it all looked like intrusion for the young couple who would have loved to have their space but today everything makes more meaning to them. Enoch later admitted that the old man was following very good examples laid down by the Scriptures.

They continued under the strict rules of Foluke's father when Enoch came home from University. At other times when he was away, they communicated through love letters and romantic gifts. Although, Enoch never experienced his father giving his mum all the care, he was not ready to lose Foluke for anything in the world, so he showered her with love and always kept to his words. Foluke was not moved by gifts, she was genuine, willing to sacrifice and loved him even when he had nothing material to give.

On the 8th of September 1967, the same year that he graduated from the University, Enoch Adejare Adeboye took Foluke Adenike Adeyokunnu to be his lawful wedded wife. The Church wedding ceremony was conducted by Rev. Jude at the Methodist Church Otapere, Ilesha, which was one of the largest Churches in Ilesha at that time. The Traditional Marriage Rites and the Court Wedding had preceded the Church Wedding. Their wedding was simple but very beautiful. The influence of Pa Jacob Adeyokunnu in the Society and the Methodist Church attracted eminent personalities from different walks of life. The reception was also simple; there was no cake to cut, no honeymoon but the guests who attended were all treated to the delicacy of very delicious pounded yam with vegetable soup and bush meat.

On the glorious Wedding day, the couple glittered in gorgeous Traditional Outfit. The bride wore the Traditional Blouse 'Buba' with the knee length Wrapper 'Iro' which was made from the prestigious fabric called 'Aso Oke'. She combined all these with very gorgeous head tie and beautiful beaded jewellery. She wore a high heel shoe that was about ten inches tall. That was the fashion in vogue at that time. The groom also wore a short sleeve traditional shirt with the pants to match; called 'buba' and 'sokoto' with a nice pair of shoes. The couple beamed with smiles as guests and family could literally see the love emanating from Enoch's eyes towards his bride. Theirs was pure love; they were both young and full of life. They had a promising future ahead of them and they had each other for it.

Chapter

5

*From Blisters
To Bliss*

The family life of Enoch and Foluke faced a lot of challenges but the faithfulness of God brought them through the storms. When they met Jesus, all their marital pains and blisters were automatically converted to marital gains and bliss. The patience God put in the couple to cope with each other trained them to be better people and they have since been complementing each other. You will read how God brought them through several storms in their marriage and above all, their love is still being rekindled each passing day. Your marriage also can turn to a palace of love, peace and unity, just keep trusting God in prayers and be patient.

SURVIVAL OF THE FITTEST

After the wedding, Enoch was faced with realities of the open world. He had to come to terms with the fact that he had to provide for his family. Now as a Graduate, he did not have to be a Grade 3 Teacher, he could teach in Secondary School. The young couple decided to start their life in the barest minimum way they could afford. They were both united and very diligent. They put all hands on deck and got a small apartment in Oke-Igbo near Ondo Township. Enoch was offered a teaching job in the new town they moved to, at Okeigbo Ifetedo Grammar School. He was employed to teach Mathematics. As usual, everyone became fond of him, ranging from the staff to the students. As he taught Mathematics, he indicated interest in sports and volunteered to be their Sports Master.

This additional portfolio made his job more interesting as he trained the pupils on the field in different sports. Being a previous gang leader in school, the children viewed him as a superstar. He definitely possessed extraordinary abilities in sports. On a particular occasion, he took the students out on competition against another school, where he met a friend. They were both excited to see each other, they got along pretty well and exchanged pleasantries. While they went on chatting, Enoch indicated his interest in furthering his education to Post Graduate Level. The particular friend was excited and told him about doing his Masters Course in the University of Lagos. Enoch was amazed at the many opportunities he could benefit so he followed it up seriously. The income he received was not usually sufficient to meet up with their responsibilities but Foluke also contributed her little quota of income.

MARITAL SQUABBLES BEGIN

Their marriage like any other was not void of initial challenges. Although Enoch and Folu were seriously in love yet they sometimes had misunderstandings. Sometimes they disagreed over issues because they had two separate backgrounds which made them think differently. For instance, it took a long time for Folu to come to terms with the attitude of her husband, who would go out all day teaching and studying, only for him to get back home and return to study. After endless waiting and longing for her husband to come home, her excitement is dashed into pieces when Adeboye walks into his room, locks up himself working Mathematical problems. That seemed absurd to Foluke and she raised several objections but when she realised he was not going to bulge, she had to live with it.

They realised that most times, at the end of the day, the squabble could have been avoided if one person had given in at every point in time. The couple also noticed that some people had reservations about the likely success of their marriage. The reason for these doubts was that they were both very young at the time they got married. Enoch was twenty five years and Foluke was nineteen and a half years. After a while, they both decided to disappoint the odd expectations of people. Enoch told his wife that it seemed some particular people were expecting them to have problems and that the solution would be for them to agree together to disappoint them. Hence, they made an agreement that both of them would never be angry at the same time. When one of them got angry, the other would keep calm and quiet; not uttering a word which could infuriate more rage.

This strategy paid out well for them because it really helped them to avoid fierce arguments despite the fact that they were not saved at the time. Another factor which helped their marriage to survive the anticipated troubles of its early days was the fact that they got married as friends. From the day they got married up till now, they have never called on a third party to settle any disputes between them.

Adeboye remembered a time when they almost broke their agreement never to get angry at the same time, which he recaps below;

> " If you take advantage of your weak moments and start praying especially in the Spirit, you will receive more strength both to continue, as well as to overcome the challenges that are lurking around you. "
>
> - Enoch Adeboye -

"When I became married, I agreed with my wife that we must not get angry at the same time. Then the devil tried to trap us one day. We were travelling from Ilesha to Lagos. Something made her angry and I knew she was right. She really had an opportunity to hit me. She was talking and I was driving. I was angry but I could not talk and there was nowhere to run. When I could not control it anymore, in order not to break our rule, I parked the car. I got down and began to walk back towards Ilesha. I left her with the baby in the car. After walking for about a mile, I got to a village where they were selling fruits and bought some. I ate some and I took the remaining to her in the car. By now she was frightened because she did not know what had happened. When she saw me coming, she became relieved and as I got into the car, I gave her the peace offering."

SEASON OF SACRIFICES

Their marriage was beautiful but they had to pull through a lot of challenges together. Though they were both working as teachers yet there was a lot of demand from their meagre income in form of support from their extended family members. Though Enoch was the last child of his father, he was the only one who was educated and was doing pretty good, so he was laden with the responsibility to assist the other members of his family in one way or the other. Also being the only son of his mother, his sisters depended on him and they were often resident in his home.

Many others such as nieces, nephews and cousins came around to live with them. Though their marriage was still young, their home was always full of relatives that depended on them. Foluke was always cooking and cleaning the house. Many of these relatives were kids left for her to cater for. Those were really hard times for the newlyweds. They had to stretch themselves thin in order to sacrifice for the wellbeing of others.

Barely two years after the marriage of Enoch and Foluke, Pa Jacob Adeyokunnu passed on. His death created another big vacuum which Mr. & Mrs. Adeboye had to rise up to. Foluke being the first child of the family had to take up the responsibility of taking care of her younger ones. So some of her siblings had to move in to live with them. For many years their home was like a boarding house with Enoch and Foluke maintaining the members of their extended families; feeding them, taking care of them and seeing to their welfare out of their own means. Enoch was always encouraging his wife to take heart and endure the hardship, which he said was temporal because their tomorrow would be alright.

POST GRADUATE STUDIES

At this time, Enoch who was always longing to climb the ladder of life to higher pedestals decided to further his education by enrolling at the University of Lagos for his Masters Degree in Hydrodynamics. Foluke remained at home to cater for her children and the other family members. The Masters program lasted for two long years. Enoch was seldom around except during the holidays. Foluke had a crowd of relatives to take care of.

Sometimes when she looked back at those days, she wondered how she survived as the caregiver for more than ten relatives including her own children. It must have been the grace of God that kept her through it all. God also used the hardness of those years to prepare her for the greater tasks which lay ahead. It was even a more difficult time for the couple but their love for each other kept them through the trials of those years.

SHATTERED HOPE OF STUDYING ABROAD

Enoch soon completed his Masters program and was able to secure an appointment. He had finally broken the jinx; he would never be a Local Farmer or even a Village Primary School Teacher. After he had concluded his Masters degree, he chose to continue to do his Doctorate so that he would achieve the highest position possible in the academic field. He had hopes of going abroad, however on scholarship because he was not financially capable of sponsoring himself abroad. He was called on to attend an interview for the Commonwealth Scholarship abroad. He was filled with excitement and joy as he prepared for the day. On the fateful day, he was seated before a panel that threw questions at him intermittently. Despite, the intimidating faces of the panel of interviewers, Enoch kept his calm and answered every question intelligently being an A student all his life. They seemed impressed until a particular interviewer that was dozing throughout the interview session suddenly woke up, and while struggling to show his relevance and presence, he threw at Enoch a question that was totally out of place. The interviewer asked Enoch, a Mathematics scholar, 'Where is Entebbe?' Adeboye was shocked at the question, so he replied abruptly that he had not applied as a Geography scholar. The moment he said that, all the other interviewers burst into laughter. The sleepy interviewer was so embarrassed and he took it out on Adeboye.

He was denied the scholarship which he had anxiously waited for. It was so painful but he did not have a choice other than look for the next available option which was to study his Doctorate Degree in the University of Lagos. At that point, he was also aiming to be the youngest Vice Chancellor in Africa. He continued pursuing his Doctorate Degree till he met the Lord.

> " The truth about divine favour is that the opinions of men do not count when God's searchlight has beamed on you. "
>
> - Enoch Adeboye -

THE CHALLENGES OF CHILDBIRTH

After few months into the marriage, God blessed the union with lovely children. Foluke's challenge in giving birth to all her children was indeed one of the greatest dilemmas which the entire family had to face. The doctors reported that due to certain bone structure in her, she could not give birth to children normally. All her children were born through the Caesarean Section procedure. Then the series of Surgeries started as Foluke bore her first son; Adeolu and then a girl; Adebolugbe. She got pregnant again and gave birth to another baby girl but the child had some challenges. She was born with jaundice and this made her handicapped. The problem of the child and the threatening Caesarean Section over the next pregnancy of Foluke was part of the main reason that brought them to Church. When Jesus saved them, they had two more sons named

Oluwadamilare and Oluwaleke, but this time, they were through normal delivery. God had delivered Foluke from the challenges of child birth.

MARRIAGE OF BLISS

After they met with the Lord, the marriage even took a more glorious turn. The same Enoch that used to lock himself up in his room working Mathematical problems became relaxed and balanced. There were times when he would try to stay on his own calculating but his wife and two older kids were always available to bring him out of the shell. He began to love and to be loved. He would share more time with his wife and their marriage took a definite turn to bliss and glory. God began to help them scale every hurdle one day at a time. Years into this marriage, Pastor Adeboye would refer to Pastor Mrs Foluke Adeboye as his 'wife and girlfriend'. When ministry work became more cumbersome, they tried to go to their meetings together but there are times that they would be in different parts of the world at the same time, doing the work of the Lord. The main ingredients that has kept them focused in such times are love, commitment and trust. They have both made a commitment to make heaven together with their family so they constantly spend quality time together. Pastor Adeboye despite his busy schedule does not abandon his wife. He constantly gives her attention, listen to her and love her. He usually teaches his leaders to love their wives and spend quality time together. They both sharpen each other as Mummy G.O takes responsibility for the welfare of the home and guests when there are great events, Pastor Enoch Adeboye takes up the spiritual responsibility and expresses unconditional love to his wife. They never com-

> " One reason why Jesus Christ is the only saviour is that of all prophets and founders of the world's religions, He alone died and resurrected. While the others are dead, He lives. "
>
> - Enoch Adeboye -

pete rather they complement each other with love.

As the children grew in such lovely environment, they were brought up with a good balance of love and discipline. Pastor Adeboye began conducting Bible Study class for his children at home. He gave them special attention and would sometimes share the same bed with them when they were on Evangelism in villages. Till date, it is obvious that their children are all taught of God and love God. Pastor Adeboye shared a testimony of his daughter many years ago,

"I remember years ago, I travelled abroad and my daughter fell sick in the college and she was brought home because she would not go to the hospital... God gave the girl an inspiration and she said, 'Mummy, please let me sleep where Daddy sleeps. Let me sleep there by your side.' She slept there and instantly, the miracle happened. Where God dwells power would dwell."

Their children also reported that they have never witnessed their parents quarrelling. By the grace of God, their marriage has survived over forty years. Their love is still waxing stronger with each passing day. When asked what has been the secret of the success of their marriage, Foluke Adeboye commented that it is pure love and honesty. She said, "I have loved my husband, I still love my husband and I will continue to love my husband". On the other hand, Enoch believes that the support of his wife has made a huge difference in the phenomenal success of his life and ministry. He once said, "I wonder how I would have coped but for the great strength of character that God has given my wife".

Up till date, if you stay around Daddy and Mummy Adeboye, it won't take few minutes before you begin to see the strong love which exists between them. This is a testimony that is worthy of mention especially in our generation of escalated divorce rates even among men and women of God.

We live in a generation where couples are at each other's faces in fights, disagreement and competition. This is not the will of God for marriage. God's plan for marriage is for couples to complement each other to accomplish destiny rather than compete. We can learn from Enoch and Foluke that only Jesus makes the difference in one's spouse and not arguments or retaliation. The fear of God will make a woman submit to her husband and make the man love his wife. Since this couple have been married for over forty years and their love is still waxing stronger, your marriage does not have to hit the rock, trust God and you will see him working things out in your favour.

Chapter

6

I Surrender All

Wow! This is the most exciting event that
happened in the story of Adeboye. This chapter
reveals God's wisdom that wrapped up a special
assignment in an unpleasant thorn in one's flesh.
This young couple found themselves being moved by
their life threatening predicaments to the altar at the
feet of Jesus. It was a dynamic shift from darkness to
light, shame to fame and dishonour to honour.
The beginning of a new phase of possibility had
dawned on him and they were ready to embrace it.
Discover the detour God used to effect
his will on Enoch Adeboye.

I'M FED UP

There is no one too deep in sin that God cannot save. The same ladies man, wine babbler, boxer and academic tycoon was soon captured by the unfailing hands of Jesus. Although Enoch was an Anglican from childhood, confirmed and permitted to take the Holy Communion, occasional Church goer yet the real person of Christ was unknown to him. He was more familiar with native doctors and spiritual diviners which were prevalent at the time. The powers of native doctors were well known to him because he had seen it in action at several instances in his growing years in Ifewara, his native village.

While lecturing in the University and striving to be the youngest Vice Chancellor in Africa, life became more challenging. He felt dissatisfied with the outward glamour he was given. He knew there was no true joy from within. All his so-called fans and lovers were soon to be discovered as users and selfish people. He knew something was missing and he needed help. Coupled with his short lived joy, disappointments from friends, he had to battle with infirmities in his body which was the regular malaria and his handicapped daughter and third child who had developed jaundice from birth. A week did not pass in their home without them having to pay a hospital bill. At the same time, his wife was faced with child delivery challenges of Caesarean Section which was extremely dangerous at the time rather than normal labour which was the order of the day. As he climbed the ladder of academic success, he was not at peace in his home. He had frequent quarrels with his wife because of the pressure of seeking solution to their continuous mishaps.

Confirming his ignorance before salvation, he said in later years, "I thank Jesus Christ that He brought me to Himself by force. I am one of those people that would never have accepted Jesus Christ if He had not used force on me. All those days, when they were asking me to accept Jesus Christ, I used to think those people who thought that I was not a Christian were fools. I used to tell them that I was born a Christian and that my father was a chief in the Church so I am going straight to Heaven. I even told them that I had bought several things for my Church and I told the Pastor not to mention my name. I used to say what else does God want me to do? They told me that with all that I had done, I was still sinning. I told them that everyone is a sinner and if God were going to destroy all sinners, nobody would be spared. I thank God today that I know some people who are not sinning. Not that we have never sinned before, but we have been saved by grace we have been washed in the blood and the past record of sin has been wiped away. I have the hope of Heaven today because I ran into trouble that could not be solved by anybody except Jesus."

ADEBOYE WITH THE WITCHDOCTOR

Days, weeks and months passed, now Enoch seemed to be reaching the end of his rope. He realised there was no other possible ways for him to continue in the same mess without seeking help. He was desperate, frustrated and pushed against the wall. Although he had looked down on people that sought help from unknown powers and spiritual means as cowards and ignorant folks that are too foolish to allow themselves to be manipulated, now nothing else mattered to him, he was ready to give it a try. As he shivered in fear and insecurity from the evils that the people that hated him would be firing at him, the constant torture of nurturing his sick child, the unending and money gulping bills from the hospital, he knew he was ready to make something happen.

> "No matter how good things are now they could be better. One turning point every child of God should crave is a movement from good to better."
>
> - Enoch Adeboye -

As a man seeking to make the change in his life and family, he was introduced to a so called "very powerful" witchdoctor with a repu-tation of infallible charms and unfailing results. Wow! Enoch was excited; thoughts of celebration and optimism flooded his mind. His problems had finally reached a stop, he would be at peace and would have more time to concentrate on attaining his vision of becoming the youngest Vice Chancellor in Africa, and of course, spend more time with the ladies that clamoured around him and eventually have more money at the clubs. Life would finally be fair on him. Little did he know that he was just at the beginning of his search for the truth.

Enoch had to bury his pride and degrees as he humbly bowed his head on meeting the witchdoctor which had his face painted with diverse colours. The witchdoctors were usually in huts (little houses of mud) with short entry doors which are intended to make you bow to the charms and gods that have been erected, as you enter in. All these were tolerable as long as his problems would end. The first point of call was that the witchdoctor convinced Enoch that his personal protection was paramount and primary. Enoch agreed and was given some voodoo (Charms) to attach to his car. To his greatest shock, the week after he had supposedly been protected from all dangers, was full of disasters. Everything went wrong and to crown it all was a series of diverse car accidents.

In his words he recapped the incident,

"I was a young man, way back in 1972, though I am still young. I bought a car. I had been driving my car without any problem in Lagos. I went home to show the car to my people and somebody asked whether the car was fortified. I asked him what he meant by be-

" Some people still think that God does not see what they do wrong in secret. This is self-deception. "
- Enoch Adeboye -

ing fortified. I told him that the car was insured. He said I did not know anything. He then took me to a man who said he would fortify the car. The man gave me three charms. One was to be tied at the bottom of the steering column. He said this was to prevent me from colliding with anything in the front. He gave me another one to tie in the boot to prevent anything from hitting me from the back. He gave me a third one that he said I should tie under my seat so that if anything happened, 'the son of man (referring to himself - Adeboye) would just disappear.' I did all he asked me to do. However, in two weeks I had three accidents. Nobody taught me before I threw the charms away."

ANOTHER WITCHDOCTOR!

After a while, he was introduced to another witchdoctor. This time, he was instructed to drag a live goat by foot, with a rope tied to its neck through major and familiar roads, where he had been hailed and admired. Although it was humiliating and degrading that a learned man of his stature and calibre had to be subjected to such state, however, he did not have a choice. He followed the directions of the witchdoctor to the letter. On arriving at the witchdoctor's house, the man was full of sores and had a broken leg. In his words he said,

"I did not learn my lessons then. Things became better still. I built a house at a very tender age. I got my Ph.D. Some people approached me that they needed to fortify me... I obliged and they took me to one herbalist. He told me to go and bring a goat and some other things. He insisted that the goat must not be brought in a car. I must lead the goat from the market to his house. Can you imagine? A lecturer in the University, struggling with a goat on the street! The goat gave me a tough time. After struggling to get the goat to him, I looked at the man who was going to fortify me and I saw his leg heavily bandaged. He saw me looking at the leg and he explained what happened. He said he was involved in a car accident in which everybody died while he only broke his leg. If the protector broke his leg, what will the one protected break?"

When Enoch thought over the two incidents, he pondered, what did he do wrong? How have the infirmities doubled in his home? What happened to the goat he had to drag through the streets to the witch doctor? Was the stubborn goat only a means of putting a month's breakfast, lunch and dinner on the witchdoctor's table? What had happened to the charm he attached to his car? Was it the cause of the accidents? Enoch did not have to ponder for long before he knew he had entered a contract of lies and deception with the devil. Then he thought logically that if the witchdoctor could not protect himself, how could he be protected? Immediately he threw all the charms away, decided never to consult any native or diabolic powers again. Now, he was stuck and back in search of the solution to his increased challenges.

WEEPING AT THE ALTAR

Now in the early months of 1973, as Enoch wallowed in his confused state, he heard rumours that God could do all things and that all he needed was to meet and know God. Well, for him, that did not sound humiliating or degrading, he could make do with that. Not long after, he was invited by his uncle, Rev Chris Fajemirokun who was aware of his confused state as well as the challenges of his health and daughter's. He was assured of the awesomeness of God and that he would be visiting God in a living Church where miraculous things happened. Was he ready for another adventure? No! However, he had no choice when he remembered that if he stopped trying, he would be swallowed up in torment. Soon, he agreed with his wife, Folu that this time they would go and check out the nearby Church. This was a Church founded by Rev Josiah Akindayomi named the Redeemed Christian Church of God situated at 9 Willoughby Street, Ebute-Meta, Lagos, Nigeria.

Preceding the coming of Enoch and Folu, God had intimated Rev Josiah Akindayomi that a well learned man would come to the Church and would eventually be his long awaited successor. On that fateful day, Enoch and Folu, who were a frustrated couple simply looking for solution to their problems sneaked into the Church and hid behind the pews observing the activities of the day. For Enoch, considering his academic prowess and sense of reasoning as an Applied Mathematics Doctorate student, he felt foolish to be sitting under a group of "stack illiterates" claiming to be searching for solution to his challenges. But for some unexplainable reason he did not walk out of the dilapidated structure called a Church, even in the heat of the Holy Ghost jamborees and Spiritual gyrations being demonstrated all around them. He also noticed that the building did not look like his idea of a Church compared to the Anglican giant Cathedrals he was used to. The only striking feature that contrasted the shabby looking structure of the Church was the sign post which read the name, constructed and spelt intelligently, The Redeemed Christian Church of God.

As the service progressed, he felt uncomfortable with the noisy worship compared to the seemingly holy, serene and quiet worship in the orthodox Churches he had sometimes worshipped. Yet he endured in anticipation of a miracle. Not long after, Rev Josiah Akindayomi, handsome, tall and dark skinned began to preach a powerful message to the congregation as he expounded the Word of God and Biblical truths. Enoch was fascinated as the preacher boasted about the miracle working power of God being able to solve any problem. Rev Josiah ministered with vibrancy and passion, totally convinced of the God he talked about. After the message, an altar call was made but Enoch and Folu were resolute not to go out to give their lives to Christ, since they did not even know what it meant or entailed in details. Before the close of the service, Rev Josiah who was full of the Holy Spirit and discernment alerted that he was excited because God had brought into the Church, his successor who would continue the work when he is gone to be with the Lord. The service ended that day and the couple still did not give their lives over to Jesus Christ. After the service, Rev Josiah and Pastor Talabi went on visitation to see Enoch and Foluke at home. This couple were surprised that it was quite unusual to be visited at home by a Pastor who had barely known them after a first visit to the Church. Well, they were excited as it showed that they were loved in the group. Rev Akindayomi and the other Pastor encouraged Bro Enoch and Sis Foluke to trust in God and continue to come to Church regularly.

Time after time, Enoch and Folu kept attending Church meetings. On that glorious day, the 29th of July 1973, Enoch being 31 years old finally accepted Jesus into his heart as his Personal Lord and Saviour. On the particular day as Rev Josiah was preaching the Word of God, the presence that surrounded Enoch felt electrified.

He sensed urgency in his spirit to make a change in his ways, he knew something had been missing in his life all along and this was his moment to receive the joy. He could hardly stay in his seat as the Word of God pierced through his hungry and weary heart. Soon an altar call was made and right before the eyes of everyone, Enoch was there at the altar, kneeling and sobbing, asking Jesus to come into his life to be his Lord and Saviour. That was the defining moment in his life. From that moment everything took a dynamic shift towards God and he was baptised by immersion. Quoting him,

"Years ago, when a problem pushed me to The Redeemed Christian Church of God, I came expecting because I was told that the prayer there was sure fire. I came and met a Church Building that looked wretched. I was a lecturer in the University and was used to going to the Cathedral. I only entered the Church because the problem that was bigger than me was pushing me. Instead of dealing with my problem, they started asking me to confess my sins and to forsake them I thought, 'These ignorant people. They do not know philosophy. They do not know sociology. They do not know psychology.' I said within me that it was not their fault but what brought me otherwise what would I be doing in the company of ignorant people like these? ... One day, it just occurred to me that something must be wrong with me. I thought within me that if they had asked for money, I would have given them. All they asked me to do was to surrender to my Maker. I was suffering, yet I was pompous. All they asked me to do was to confess and repent of my sins. That day I surrendered. The Almighty God washed me in His Blood and I became a brand new creature this was the turning point in my own life."

OH WHAT A JOY

Wow! Enoch had just received a fresh fire and he could not be stopped. He felt different and elated. The fears, doubts and insecurity that had accompanied him over the years had evaporated into thin air. He felt he was now on his feet. One of the unexplainable differences he felt was a gentle peace and joy in his heart. As he had turned a new leaf, he bid goodbye to the company of wine bibbers and the line of ladies that used to sur-round him. He began to discover the true in-ner beauty that God had embedded in his wife. Oh! Love began to grow and glow in their home. As things began to change inside Enoch, the regular sicknesses he encountered began to fade away.

> " If you do not learn from the fall of your predecessors, you will fall where they fell. "
> - Enoch Adeboye -

GROWING WITH ZEAL

Enoch knew he could not hide such joy to himself, he felt like tell-ing it to the world like someone eager to show off a great treasure. First, he wanted to know more about the source of this joy, so he dusted his Bible and began to read it day by day. The zeal in him was so great that a day did not pass without him studying the Word of God as well as telling someone about Jesus. He was hungry to know the Bible more when he realised although he had knowledge in the area of academics, he knew next to nothing about God, even the local illiterate traders were vast in the things of God. That was a big challenge to him who could write and read anything fluently.

He said later after many years,

"The first time I heard a brother prophesy in a meeting, I was a young Christian then so I touched the fellow who took me to the meeting and asked, 'When did God say that? I did not hear any-thing.' The fellow asked me to keep quiet because God was talking. That day I made up my mind that I must hear God talk too."

Adeboye was very inquisitive and wanted to know everything about God. He went to meet Rev Josiah, who was his mentor at the time and explained his concerns. He pleaded with the clergy to spare him at least one hour every week for personal teaching and Bible Study where it would be just both of them and he would have the freedom to ask questions without feeling embarrassed with anyone's presence. Enoch made this request in wisdom because he knew he had some questions that if asked in public might sound too elementary or even stupid. So if the questions were any of the two, then it would be easier for him to make adjustments and corrections in his ideologies and philosophies while he learnt from his Pastor privately.

TEACH ME TO PRAY

Another strategy he applied was to find a particular brother in the Church every service and sit next to him. The idea behind that was because he did not really know how and what to say in prayers, so sitting close to this brother would gear him up. He could not find the right words to utter in prayer since he was new in practical Christianity, but he was smart enough to come early and sit next to the brother. He had admired the mannerism, fervency and passion with which the brother prayed so when a prayer was called, he would secretly be listening to the words of the brother's prayers and would be repeating the same thing loudly with the same agility and vibrancy without the brother's knowledge. He noticed that the brother would keep praising and thanking God for close to 55 minutes out of a one hour prayer. That was how he learnt to pray until he could stand on his feet. Till date, he follows the same pattern of prayer. His prayers are filled with thanksgivings and praises to God.

NOW THAT YOU BELIEVE

Pastor Akindayomi continued to tutor Adeboye in his new found faith. He was encouraged to start winning souls for Jesus. He was trained to follow Jesus in all circumstances. Although they came there looking for miracles, they were encouraged to know the miracle Worker Himself. They had to follow Jesus in all circumstances, whether in the rain or fire. The new couple would come to Church and join the other believers as they sang.

Over 30 years after the salvation experience Pastor Adeboye recalls, "When I was a younger Christian, we sang songs like, 'I want everybody to know Jesus loves every soul. My life I will give as long as I live, to let everybody to know...' We wanted to serve Jesus. This was our passion and our joy. We wanted to win souls. At that time we were more interested in what we could do for Him than what we could get from Him. We believed He had done enough in saving our souls. We wanted people to know that Jesus loves every soul."

As Adeboye grew by the day, the power of God continued to rest on him. He grew in wisdom and counsel. One day, he was told two stories about the importance of him sharing the gospel to the world.

The first story was about a newlywed couple that were so zealous for God. On a particular day, they went on Evangelism and got to a place with a solid brick high fence with iron gates. With the intention of preaching to the people in there, they knocked and knocked till a gateman peeped through the gate and told them they were in a restricted area because the inhabitants of the place are lepers in hundreds. They were unmoved as they insisted that they would still want to go in. The gateman quickly reminded them that anyone that was let in would not be allowed to go out. The couple felt even more excited and said, Jesus only told them to 'Go', He did not talk about coming back which meant, it would be taken care of, if there was a need. The souls in the lepers colony was more important to them than their wellbeing, so they persuaded the gateman and they were let in not minding getting infected with leprosy as long as souls were saved.

The second story was about a Caucasian who came to evangelise in Africa. She chose a rural community with many villages, she began reaching out to the villages and many souls were saved, the people were happy and excited. Then she inquired if there was any other surrounding village she had not witnessed. The people told her there was a village but there was no way for her to get there. She marvelled and the people told her no one crosses from their village to the other side because in between the villages was a jungle full of lions. The lady insisted she would go and then an old man volunteered to go with her, everyone was amazed and wondered his reason because he was too frail, he definitely would not be able to fight the lions. The man responded that he learnt from his late father who was a hunter that lions are usually together and they kill only when they are hungry. He said, his rationale for volunteering to go was not to defend the woman but to go ahead of her so that he could be eaten by the lions first. Then after the lions must have been full, the woman would go through the jungle to the other village, free of attack.

> " The venom of serpents and poison of scorpions against you will lose their power if only you can serve the Lord acceptably. "
> - Enoch Adeboye -

I MUST TELL SOMEBODY ABOUT JESUS

From the moment Adeboye got saved, God began to do several things in his life. It was a series of testimony week after week. So he could hardly wait till Sundays to share the testimonies of the things that happened in the week. Whenever there was testimony time in the Church, Adeboye's hands were always up. He gave a testimony every week. One day he raised his hands to give a testimony but Pa Josiah asked him to put his hands down, he felt hurt but obeyed. Another week he raised his hands for testimony and the same thing happened. He felt hurt again but later, the Holy Spirit convicted him to be humble and submissive to his spiritual father and that he was going through a training process.

With the spiritual guidance of Pa Josiah, Adeboye became addicted to preaching the gospel of Jesus to people outside the Church. He became an addicted soul winner. He never let a day pass without him winning a soul for Jesus. It became so much that if he remembered that he had not witnessed Jesus to someone in a day, he would jump out of his sleep at night and rush to the streets, looking for someone to tell about Jesus. This was one of the most interesting aspects of the conversion of Adeboye. He had the overwhelming zeal to tell everyone he met about Jesus. At other times, he visited the prisons, hospitals and less privileged people. Since he was still working as a lecturer, he shared the gospel with his students and lecturers. Everyone in his sphere of influence knew something had happened to him. Some accepted Jesus and some declined but he was never ashamed or discouraged, he continued to preach to his family members and even his neighbours. Everyone knew something had happened to him. When the fire became unbearably too hot for him to hold, he began a small fellowship which included his personal staff, secretary, cleaner, driver, janitor and the likes. Soon many were saved as more staff joined and their lives also took a definite turn to Jesus.

Enoch was excited with the great things that was happening in the fellowship he started in University of Lagos so he organised another monthly staff fellowship in University of Ibadan (about 60 miles away) and University of Ife (about 120 Miles away). He kept sharing the Word of God he had learnt with the fellowships and God was faithful, confirming His words.

SCHOOL ON FIRE

Some members of his Lagos fellowship saved the whole University from a disaster. Some secret cult members who were the students decided to set the whole school in flames. The perpetrators had bought several gallons of petrol to perfect their wicked act, and they were going to start from the Senate Building. Enoch Adeboye was out of town when the news reached some of his followers. They decided to put the things he had taught them about God into practice so that they would save their school from fire. Adeboye's disciples called themselves together and began to pray fervently. They only woke up the next morning to realise the cultists could not perform their evil act. God had caused a deep sleep to fall on all the evil perpetrators at their agreed place of meeting. When they woke up, the day had dawned and they began to argue and fight each other and they left in a big confusion. This was how the University was saved from the device of these Cultists.

Chapter

7

Yes Lord, Yes!

As it is popularly said that God does not 'call the qualified', he 'qualifies the called' is a true example in the life of Enoch Adejare Adeboye. Flipping through some scenes of his life through this book reveals that starting from his background to the point he met Jesus, he was not the perfect man for any work that involved the saving of other people's souls. However, our standards are different from God's standard and His ways are different from our ways. Watch God turn a man from a wrong way to a right way just to favour a righteous course and protect His interest.

1 Samuel 16:7b "for the LORD seeth not as man seeth, for man looketh on the outward appearance but the LORD looketh on the heart."

Chapter

7

Yes
Lord,
Yes!

MY FIRST OUTSTANDING SACRIFICE

Brother Adeboye had joined the workers in the Church and he enjoyed the service at the feet of Jesus. At the same time, he was very cautious to heed to all the instructions his Pastor and Mentor gave. He took notes in the Church and marked out every important and striking passages of the Bible that was referred to in the Church. His attention was apt as he watched and listened to Rev Josiah while ministering. On getting home, he usually went back to his notes and studied the Word of God. Although he had so many Mathematical formulas in his memory, he found a prime place for Bible verses in his heart. He memorised the scriptures daily quoting them as he continued his day to day activities and referred to them in his Bible when he got it muddled up.

On a particular Sunday, they came to Church as usual, prayed and worshipped God and heard the Word of God. In the course of the service, the Spirit of the Lord led Rev Josiah Akindayomi to give a strange instruction in order to test the obedience of his Pastors, associates and workers. It was a season of a great financial need in the Church, the members had outgrown the building, and hence they were ready for an expansion. Pa Josiah Akindayomi who was in his mid-sixties instructed every worker of the Church to go to their banks and savings, empty their accounts, and bring the funds to Church the next Sunday trusting God to see them through their other needs as they arose. Everyone went home with jubilation for the mighty promises of God to them.

Monday morning came, Bro Enoch and Sis Folu Adeboye could hardly sleep throughout the night in urgency to get to the bank and withdraw all their savings in obedience to the word of the man of God. They both emptied their bank accounts and prepared it to give to the Lord. The week passed and everyone was back in Church the following Sunday, the usual celebrations began and Pa Akindayomi was back on the altar, soon he asked those who had heeded to the last week's instruction to raise their hands.

To the greatest amazement of the congregation, no one raised any hands up except Bro Enoch and Sister Folu Adeboye. Not even the Pastors, ministers or other workers that Brother Adeboye looked up to as "hyper spiritual" had emptied their accounts to help the work of God. He thought it was automatic that everyone would and should obey the Word of God, if they claimed to love God. My God! Adeboye thought for a minute.

The couple were dazed and thought they had become overzealous and fanatical about their belief in Jesus. Rev Josiah could read the embarrassment written all over their faces and urged Brother Adeboye not to feel foolish for doing the right thing because he is the "chosen one". The words of the man of God made the couple feel a bit relieved, although being the "chosen one" did not make much sense to them at the time but of course, it sounded like a good compliment for their obedience and sacrifice. That was another confirmation to Pa Josiah Akindayomi that God's hands were on Enoch Adeboye and he is the God-ordained successor for him to continue to lead the Redeemed Christian Church of God after he is gone.

THE PRAYER GOD DID NOT ANSWER

As Brother Adeboye as fondly called by the brethren at the time, continued in prayer and the Word of God, his life continued to take a progressive move. He was willing to spread the good news at whatever cost. He had no restraints. Everyone soon noticed his zeal towards the things of God including, Rev Josiah who was mentoring him. As he never missed a Church service, he was chosen to interpret the messages from Yoruba (the native language of Rev Josiah) into English as the Pastor preached in all his meetings. This was aimed at attracting other non-Yoruba speaking people and literate members to the wonderful things God was doing in the Church.

Soon, Bro Adeboye became extremely active and fervent in the things of God and in the Church. Despite his tight schedule of lecturing in the University and rigours of pursuing his degree, he was the first to get to the Church Services. The gifts of God began to mark him as outstanding amongst many. After few months, he was informed that he was going to be ordained as a Pastor. At that point, he went home and discussed with his wife, Sister Folu. After much examination of the offer, they both concluded that they were not ready for such a position for so many reasons. However, they knew the only way they could convince the man of God not to ordain Brother Adeboye as a Pastor was to let God stop him. Since they had now grown to a particular level in God, they decided to go on a fourteen days fasting and intense prayer asking God to stop Rev Josiah from ordaining Brother Adeboye. After the series of prayer and fasting, they felt at ease believing that God would let Rev Josiah change his mind. Alas, to their greatest surprise, God did not seem to answer that prayer as Brother Adeboye and four others were called out on

> " If God cannot entrust you with secrets, you are ill-prepared for ministry. "
> - Enoch Adeboye -

the 14th of September 1975 and ordained as Reverend Doctors. Now, in later years, Pastor Adeboye reflects,

"Under no circumstance would I have become a Pastor not to talk of a General Overseer if God were not the Almighty. There is no way you can fight against this God and win. That is something everybody should know because left to me I did not want to have anything to do with priesthood. When I knew that I was going to be ordained a Pastor, my wife and I fasted for fourteen days praying that God would change His mind. At that time as a lecturer in the University, I had done a little human management because of the rapid promotion that God gave me. I had to act for my head of department while he was away and I found out that the most difficult creatures to handle are human beings. Even in the University system, you have an element of what I call 'power to enforce whatever you say', but in the Church, it is different. I have always said that the power which the Pastor has is the power given to him by God principally but also mainly by the congregation."

> " Relocating out of God's will takes you outside of your place of visitation. "
> - Enoch Adeboye -

LET'S SILENCE THE GODS

In 1977, as his staff fellowship grew, Pastor Adeboye had the urge to replicate the same time in his home town in Ifewara. Hence, he leased a cocoa produce warehouse there which was used as a branch of the Redeemed Christian Church of God. In the same year, he started an outreach in contrast to the pre-eminent festival that had swept the nation called "Festac 77" (Festival of African Arts and Culture). He felt the festival was diabolic and a mismanagement of funds and resources because it encouraged honouring the dead native gods, which he was sure were dead, dumb and powerless.

He chose to counter this movement with a four days Congress of Christians praising, praying and honouring the true and living God which he served. The event held in Osun State between the 7th – 11th of April 1977. The meetings were splendid as people turned up, the Spirit of God took over as they worshipped in celebration to God, the Word of God was shared, prayers were made and souls were converted to God. That was the beginning of a revival in the neighbourhood. The people that witnessed the meetings were so blessed and they were ready that more of the programmes should be held on a regular basis in neighbouring towns. Pastor Adeboye who recognised he was under authority sought permission from Rev Akindayomi. He was granted the permission because God had already informed Rev Akindayomi several years before that the man who will succeed him, that is, Pastor Adeboye, would be so zealous and would take initiative moves to advance the work of God. Everything happening was a fulfilment of prophecy.

FROM THE PULPIT TO A PIT

The enemy being aware of God's hands on Pastor Adeboye tried to terminate his life before the outburst of the glory but it was simply impossible. As the zeal of God consumed Enoch Adeboye, he went on a missionary trip to a city called Ilorin. Ilorin is a city in Kwara State and is about 200 miles from Lagos, approximately 4-5 hours drive. He had to minister in a crusade, which he did. The power of God was evident and souls were saved, healing and several remarkable miracles happened. The people were excited and their lives were changed. The crusade was life transforming not just for those who attended but also for Enoch who ministered there. After the great surprises God gave him at the crusade, he could not keep the news to himself, he rushed back to Lagos to share it with his friend. As he approached his friend's place with sister Folu who was heavily pregnant at the time, they got to a construction site which they had to cross. Sister Folu crossed over the open pit safely but as Pastor Adeboye was going to cross, he missed his steps and fell in the big pit with a bang. That was a big accident for Adeboye and he needed to stay still for a while to regain his consciousness. Suddenly, he heard the loud scream and shouts of his wife who was frightened. It occurred to him that he would not want his wife to get too agitated because of her health condition at the time. He also thought, she would attract crowds and it would be a shameful thing to see the preacher and University Professor helpless in a

> " If you have all the wealth in the world, without ministering to those you were destined to bless, you cannot be fulfilled. "
>
> - Enoch Adeboye

pit. In splits of seconds, he jumped up and walked a few meters to his friend's place where he helplessly collapsed and fainted. Pandemonium struck between Sister Folu and his friend, and they both called for help and he was miraculously resuscitated.

ESCAPE OF DEATH IN ILORIN

Later on, he made another trip to Ilorin. He was chauffeur driven and as he sat at the back meditating, something strange happened. The devil was at it again, he wanted to terminate Adeboye. They had approached a very narrow bridge on top speed before they realised another vehicle, an eighteen wheel truck was coming on the single lane as well and at a high speed. The truck was so close and was about to crush them when Adeboye and his driver shouted 'Jesus!' It was so sure that they would have been crushed as they would have been expecting to hear the sonorous voices of the angels singing halleluyah in heaven, but God is faithful. The next thing they realised was that they had reached the other side of the road and the truck had passed. Both the driver and Adeboye till date cannot give accounts of what happened in between the time the truck approached them and when they got to the other side. The only way Pastor Adeboye could explain the feeling after the incident is that they were both shaking like banana leaves as they drove silently and extremely cautious to their destination.

TOILET STUDY

Adeboye was so committed to studying more in the Bible. In 1977, he went for a Conference in Nairobi, Kenya. The Conference was very interesting but busy because it was packed with several teaching materials. Everyone was to pay attention and attend all the sessions so the only time attendees had to themselves was the time they came back to their hostels. People would familiarise, meet new people and chat with others. When Adeboye realised that every time he tried to read the study materials they got or even the Bible, there were too many distractions. He got so desperate to pray, study the Bible and read the study notes that he resolved into retiring to the toilet. He would stay in the toilet for long hours till he finishes his prayers and study. This was a desperate measure to keep himself separated away from fruitless activities.

In the conference, he also had this revelation. At this time, he was a Holiness Preacher and he thought he was on fire for God, sparkling clean until he had the vision. While there was a music ministration in the conference, God opened Pastor Adeboye's eyes and he found himself before the giant throne room of God. He saw angels on his right side and when he looked forward, someone sat on the throne. He noticed he was standing on a rug-like object like a circle, he also realised he was also stack naked. He looked so dirty like someone who had just been brought out of a pit latrine or toilet full of faeces. When he moved right and left, the angels moved back and the one that sat on the throne did not say anything. He returned to his consciousness, then he knew he had seen a vision and he denoted that God wanted him to clean up all his ways and leave totally holy. He made up his mind that the next time he would appear before the throne, he would go clean.

BIBLICAL EQUATION

Pastor Adeboye saw God intervene in every sphere of his life. He did not leave anything unattended or any stone unturned. From the moment he accepted Jesus into his life, everything took a turn around and he let Jesus decide the most tiniest issues of his life. Some time earlier, he was scheduled to finalise his Doctorate Degree. So he picked a Mathematical Equation to solve that would eventually qualify him. He thought it was going to be an easy one until he found it almost impossible to solve the problem he chose. He had spent a lot of time but the Mathematical problem seemed more difficult. It was however too late to change his chosen equation and he was also running late on time. Day after day, he tried it out but it seemed the harder he tried to solve it, the more difficult and impossible the equation got. He then handed everything over to God and picked his Bible to study. As he chose a portion to study, he bumped into the story of the Red Sea and the Children of Israel. As he dwelt on the passage, he got thrilled when he read how the sea parted into two sides and the Children of Israel passed in the middle. Instantly, the Holy Spirit ministered to him that the way God parted the Red Sea was the solution to the Mathematical Problem. He quickly picked the Mathematical Equation he had been trying to solve for a long time but this time, the answer was on his table. He used the Biblical equation of the sea parting into two sides, so he parted the Mathematical Problem into two parts, arranged his formula into two parts, and he went on and on working it out gradually till the problem was totally solved. He got so excited on how God used a Biblical Situation to solve his Mathematical Equation.

WHY SHOULD I TITHE?

His walk with God grew day by day as God spoke to him clearer. There was nothing too much for Pastor Adeboye to do or give to God. However, he realised he had not fully understood a major issue of paying his tithe, that is, a tenth of his income to God. He was not familiar with such an act and he found it a lot confusing. He continued coming to Church but being a mathematician,

" The best place to be is where God wants you to be at any point in time. "
- Enoch Adeboye -

he had made calculations for his income and every bit of it was tagged. On a certain occasion, he called on Rev Josiah Akindayomi and asked to get a full teaching on the issue of paying tithes. He went home and confirmed all he was taught. After several battles in his Mathematical mind, he consented to paying his tithe because God instructed Christians and he also loved the Lord.

His first tithe was paid on a particular Sunday. Soon he heard God ask him if he was ready to be blessed. He responded positively. God told him to be ready for hard work and prosperity. He was sure set to see God do the extra ordinary. He was stunned when he resumed to office on Monday, only to receive a miracle. The Dean of his Faculty called him and said he had been recommended as a good teacher of Mathematics. Adeboye was delighted. The next statement of the Dean, that the Lagos Anglican Girls Grammar School needed a Mathematics Teacher and that he should go there, almost angered Adeboye. He was a University lecturer, how could the Dean tell him to go and teach in a Grammar School? He almost responded but felt a restraint so he agreed to go. When he got to the Grammar School, he met the principal who asked the number of hours he would be willing to spare. He told them but got overwhelmed when he realised his pay for 6 hours in the Grammar School was more than what he earned as a lecturer. About a month later, he got another call to CMS Grammar School; they paid him very well as well. By that time, his previous earning had doubled with the income from just the two schools. Again, another friend of his, Professor Adebayo Mokuolu had a school. When the professor heard, he was upset that Adeboye was teaching in schools of people he did not know and was not teaching in his school, being a good friend of his and he desperately needed a Mathematics Teacher. This was how his earnings multiplied drastically. At this point, his faith was built and knew that paying his tithe regularly pleased God.

What will be your answer when the Lord calls you? You better decide to give God the wheels of your life and surrender totally to His leading. Let your answer be "Yes Lord, Yes!"

Chapter

8

The Elijah And His Elisha

Until you serve, you might not be served! The great
Legend of Faith being reviewed through the pages of
this book was not just dropped from heaven, he was
handpicked by God and committed to a higher authority
to be trained. He learned to serve without grudge,
query or limitations. This man poured water on the hands
of his predecessor, received rebukes and sharpened his
innate leadership qualities as an Elisha under the tutelage
of an Elijah.

Chapter

8

*The Elijah
And
His Elisha*

There is no better relationship than that of the Biblical Elijah and Elisha that would describe the bond that existed between Enoch Adejare Adeboye and Pa Josiah Akindayomi. Their meeting, bonding, separation goes beyond the ordinary, excels human calculations and supersedes what mundane minds can paint with the brush of their imagination or utter with the insufficient terms called words. They were a pair made from heaven to touch the world.

PA JOSIAH AKINDAYOMI
CALLED FOR A PURPOSE

Pa Akindayomi was born on July 5, 1909, which made him a few weeks to sixty four years old when he set his eyes on Enoch Adeboye for the first time. He was a tall, dark, well built and good looking grey-headed man. He was firm and blunt. For everyone that met him, there was a remarkable story they had to tell. He was a very

> " Kingdom service is a sickness extractor. The more you serve, the healthier you live. "
> - Enoch Adeboye -

kind man that took the burdens of others on himself. Besides all his physical attributes, he was spiritually sound in teachings, prayers and fasting. Although he was not educated, yet he had an unquenchable thirst for knowledge and advancement.

At the age of eighteen, he signed up to learn English Alphabets but it did not last too long. He joined the Church Missionary Society (C.M.S), an Anglican Church that flooded the country at the time. It was in the C.M.S Church that he got baptised. In quest for spiritual upliftment, at the age of 22, he joined another group that was vibrant called the Cherubim and the Seraphim movements. It was said that the Church was very good and it stood on the truth as at that time but later were said to have deviated into controversial and questionable doctrines.

YES LORD, I CHOOSE TO OBEY

At the age of 24, he heard the first call to be God's servant but for seven years, he ignored the call until the Lord frustrated him in his other endeavours. He did not yield to the call of God in those seven years but preferred to continue his farming which seemed more financially secure than becoming a poor Pastor. At last, he had to surrender when he had a dream and saw an old man scratch his legs with fingernails, only to wake up and find a big sore on the same leg. He was shocked as the wound enlarged and deepened within few weeks till his bones were visible to people. In the middle of his torment with the sore, this young 31 year old man heard God call him again. This time, he was pushed to the wall and immediately responded to the call of God.

On July 10, 1940, Josiah left his native land to another town where

God had directed him about 40miles away called Ile-Ife. On his journey, he could miraculously read and understand some specific scriptures without any previous knowledge of reading or writing in any language. He encountered so many miraculous experiences on the way. On getting there, the Lord directed him to go back and burn up his bridges in his native town, Ondo, he had to go and sell all his belongings, offset his bills and give up his room in his father's house because he would never need it. When he got back to his native town on July 24, 1940, his mother was shocked to see him carry out all those instructions. For a while, she assumed he had gone insane but what could the old woman do? She had to give up to fate. Josiah voluntarily served in the Cherubim and Seraphim Church till 1947 when the Church began to go to the cemetery to consult the dead. This was heretical to Josiah so he began to organise Bible study meetings correcting the members and preaching the truth. This only lasted till 1952 when he was excommunicated from the Church.

TRUTH AT LAST

In the year 1952, when God was preparing Adeboye who was only a ten years old little boy in the backside of a desert, God simultaneously gave Pa Josiah Akindayomi a transforming experience. Josiah's departure from the Cherubim and Seraphim movement was his first salvation decision. Many other sacrifices had to follow, he knew he had met the true and living God so he put away the 'prophet' title he had gotten from the previous Church, he stopped the burning of candles and discarded the white garment.

He continued his small Bible Study at 9 Willoughby Street, Ebute -Meta where only a handful of people came. It did not bother him for the joy he had just received of the true light made him vivacious. He led many that came for the Bible Study to accept Jesus as their Lord and Saviour since he had done the same. Another amazing change he made was restitution; he had three wives, of which one had left; now he was left with two. After his salvation experience, he explained to the wife that he had accepted Jesus and he was a changed man, so after much persuasions and prayer, the wife decided to leave, so he stayed with the first wife, Esther till his death. The fellowship grew gradually and was called the Apostolic Faith of South Africa although the Church had nothing to do with South Africa, it was later changed to Apostolic Faith Mission of West Africa and finally God gave him the name, The Redeemed Christian Church of God. The Church continued to grow gradually until the day Enoch Adeboye and Josiah Akindayomi met, then destiny took place.

DESTINY HAPPENED

In 1941, the year before Enoch Adejare Adeboye was born, God spoke to Josiah Akindayomi that He would take him to the land of the white men regarding the work of the gospel. This looked like an impossible promise to Pa Josiah because he was uneducated, couldn't speak or write the white man's language – English. To make it worse, he was young, unexposed and had not even started his Bible Study Fellowship. He was still trying to find the true light of God so how on earth could he possibly go abroad with all these negatives? Little did he know that, the answer to his puzzles was being packaged and sent to the earth in the form of Adeboye.

God had told Pa Josiah Akindayomi about Pastor Adeboye for over twenty (20) years before they met. So he knew him the moment he set his eyes on him, he knew the description God gave him and it fitted perfectly, he knew Adeboye was his successor and the next General Overseer of The Redeemed Christian Church of God. The most commendable aspect was that Pa Akindayomi, for those twenty years did not cease to tell his Pastors, ministers, members and whoever cared to know that there was no need to contend over who will take over from him because the leader for the Church and his successor was not yet among them. God showed him a vision of the man that will take over the leadership those two decades ago. He had been telling his Pastors that the man would be highly educated, the same height as him, the same stature so much that if he would wear his clothes, it would fit perfectly. God also said his successor would have become vibrant and would take some initiatives about doing spectacular things for God. As this old man continued to tell his Pastors, 'The leader of this Church for tomorrow is not yet among us', some of his followers who were power seekers left the Church while some others thought he would eventually change his mind.

Destiny happened on that faithful day Adeboye walked into the Church desperately looking for a solution to his mountain of problems. He did not know that he was the solution to the mountain of the questions in the heart of Rev Josiah. The moment, their eyes met, something leaped in Rev Josiah, he knew Destiny had just happened, Elisha had just met Elijah.

> " There are good and bad ways of doing a thing. Never adopt bad or questionable measures for spiritual assignments. "
>
> - Enoch Adeboye -

This was the reason Rev Josiah gave the Adeboyes' a courtesy visit in their home the first day they came to the Church.

MISSION TO ISRAEL

Pa Josiah Akindayomi went on a holy pilgrimage to Israel in 1975 along with Pastor Igbekoyi who was one of his assistants. On his way, he had a stop-over in Rome where he was privileged to meet the reigning pope who gave him an audience. On getting to Israel, he visited several places of interest where Jesus walked. When he was known as a Church leader from Africa, he was given a Jerusalem

Pilgrimage outfit which included a white gown, a white veil and hand gloves. It was indeed a transforming experience for the grey headed old preacher. While there, he had received further instructions and quickening on the great move of God that would happen in the Church. God made several promises to him, some of which are evident today. Also the Lord quickened him on the Mount of Transfiguration and told him to start tidying things up because Adeboye, the leader of tomorrow would soon take over. He was excited to have heard God so clearly. It was on his return that he ordained Adeboye as Reverend Doctor.

THE BONDING OF THE PROPHETS

The new Pastor Adeboye and interpreter for Rev Josiah was still bubbling in the euphoria of knowing God more. He was still eager to learn every little bit of thing he could. Although he had obtained his doctorate degree, he still had to battle with his full time lecturing job which was putting good food on his table. As much as Adeboye could not wait to be taught by Rev Akindayomi, Rev Akindayomi also could not wait to pour his heart out and mentor Adeboye since he was aware that Adeboye would be his successor.

As he continued as Pa Akindayomi's interpreter, their relationship increased and they bonded even more as father to son and mentor to protégée. Soon, the old grey headed prophet could no longer hide the level of authority God was positioning his young prophet into, so Adeboye was drastically promoted to the Elders Fellowship. This position fetched him the title 'young elder' since his age at the time did not qualify him for that fellowship.

The two prophets bonded seriously so much that Pa Akindayomi would not go and minister anywhere without taking his son, Adeboye along. Protégé Adeboye was very submissive and teachable, as he followed his mentor around interpreting for him. When they returned from public meetings, they stayed together in lengthy hours of tutoring and heartfelt instructions. Pa Josiah was a phenomenal father, he would encourage Adeboye to prepare sermons notes, ask him to preach it to him and make corrections where necessary. Gradually the spirit and power of God on the life of Rev Josiah began to rub off on Adeboye. Their bond was like that of Elijah and Elisha, as Adeboye served without hesitation or grudge, the anointing of God fell on him the more. They would engage in long hours of prayers so much that Adeboye was said to have a personal room in the house of Pa Akindayomi since they stayed up sometimes till very late in the night and even into the break of day at other times. Pa Akindayomi's wife would sometimes prepare their dinner waiting for them to finish their long hours of discussions. She eventually would go to bed after an endless wait and wake up the next morning to find the food still untouched. However, no one has details of the last instructions of Pa Akindayomi but we can guess the great explosions and exploits we see today are fruits of those pressing hours.

MAN COVERED WITH LEPROSY

Anytime Pa Akindayomi had to go round visiting the branches of his Church, he would ask Pastor Adeboye to come with him. They went and encouraged the people at different intervals. On one of their trips, they travelled all the way to settle a dispute between the Parish Leader and some Members. The Parish was at Oshogbo, Oyo State (about 3-4 hours drive). When they got there, Pa Akindayomi called the leader into a meeting and pleaded with him as he tried to resolve the issue. He appealed to the man to allow peace to reign instead of fighting and revelling. It looked like the gentler Pa Josiah was as he begged, the more

" One reason many continuously make mistakes is because of the spirit of error. "

- Enoch Adeboye -

aggressive and unrepentant the Parish Leader got. He began to talk down the old man and he made a big scene, threatening to break away from the Church. Everyone told him he was going too far but he remained adamant and disrespectful to the Man of God.

Pastor Adeboye watched the scenario and was dazed at the humility and meekness Pa Akindayomi demonstrated despite all the insults from a junior minister. They returned to Lagos and soon it was reported to them that as soon as they left, before the day was over, the rebellious minister was covered with leprosy from head to toe. People came to beg Pa Akindayomi in Lagos to forgive the young minister, but Pa Akindayomi told them the truth that he knew nothing about the leprosy, it was God's judgement on the man.

As Enoch watched God fight for Pa Akindayomi, God has been faithful to him as well. The same grace has been replicated in the life of Pastor Adeboye as many that maltreat and cheat him have been punished by God even without his knowledge.

As he grew under the tutelage of Pa Akindayomi, special commendable character traits robbed off. He learnt to be a servant leader, he saw by example how the old man related with people in humility and sobriety. Soon the same spirit of faith became evident in the life of Pastor Adeboye. He unconsciously had taken after the footsteps of his father, the anointing rubbed off on him and he was trained in the way of God. As they grew together, Pastor Adeboye began to exercise his faith, praying for members of his household that had minor sicknesses like headaches and the like. He prayed and God healed, he gradually began to grow in faith as he prayed for more sick people outside his house. There were times he was confronted with serious situations that he could not handle, he would retreat to his mentor to get further instructions or allow the older prophet to handle the situation while he watched. He also learnt how to pray fervently and fast from Pa Akindayomi. His faith continued to grow daily and God took the glory.

Chapter

9

*The Annointed
Becomes
Appointed*

It is of extreme value when a work is passed to the right hands.
It marks the beginning of a new movement, the breeding
of a new generation and harvest of a colourful future.
God's selection of his vessel always contradicts our choices.
This is because He always has an intention.
Here, we read on the benefits of choosing God's man and the
importance of transferring the mantle of leadership to the right
hands. When passing the baton in a race, sentiments are
not considered, pass it to the right man, then win the race!

*The
Annointed
Becomes
Appointed*

TRANSFER OF MANTLE

After young elder Adeboye had fulfilled all prophecies including starting the Massive Evangelistic Outreach called 'Congress' in 1977, Rev Josiah knew time was running out and he needed to pour all he could into Pastor Adeboye. Although it was no longer a secret that Pastor Adeboye was the successor for Pa Akindayomi, yet the reality began to dawn on the old man as the days went by. He had to break the news formally to Adeboye, though he knew it was not going to be easy because Adeboye was now a Doctor of Mathematics, his intelligence was exceptional. One thing was sure, Adeboye loved the Lord and would obey the voice of God when given an instruction to carry out.

On the other hand, the Lord had also told Adeboye that he would be taking over from Pa Akindayomi. The Lord told him in a humorous way. According to him, he said he was in the bush easing himself when God asked him who he thought could take over the leadership of the Church. He quickly named three senior ministers that were elderly and mature. He thought they seemed fit as elders to wear the leadership shoes since they were there long enough and are already familiar with the Church. As he responded, he concluded and said to himself 'what is my business anyway about who takes over?' Suddenly, he heard God ask him, 'What about you?' That question came on a bit strong on the young man because he had his goals and ambitions which he was so careful to guard jealously. However, he remained silent as he was sceptical about the answer God gave him.

" It's not enough to see or touch miracles. Ask God to cause you to experience and carry miracles wherever you go. "
- Enoch Adeboye -

MISSIONARY TRIP TO TULSA, OKLAHOMA

In 1979, the year Pa Akindayomi turned 70 years old, he decided to make another trip outside the shores of his country. He chose to go to a Kenneth Hagin Camp Meeting which was to hold in Tulsa Oklahoma, United States of America. He went with an entourage and they were six in number. It was a ten days trip and they resided at Downtown Hotel. They were hosted by Rev Stephen Rathod, an American studying in Tulsa, Oklahoma who took them round to Restaurants, Shopping Malls, the Convention Centre and their Hotels.

The Camp Meeting ended on a Saturday, so they decided to go to a Church on Sunday. When they got to the programme, it was interesting and the preacher ministered powerfully. Since Pa Akindayomi was illiterate, Pastor Adeboye had to interpret the message to him at different intervals. Suddenly, the preacher walked to Pa Josiah and began to prophesy directly to him, 'Thus saith the Lord, what I told you several years ago will soon be fulfilled'. Then he turned back and continued preaching. Pa Josiah was surprised and asked Pastor Adeboye to interpret the prophetic word the preacher said to him. It was not so easy for Pastor Adeboye to quickly understand the American accent the preacher spoke with but he did this time. So he told his spiritual father that he would tell him the message when they get home. When they got home, Pastor Adeboye told the old man the message, then he (Pa Josiah) broke down in tears. When asked the reason for the sudden tears, he said the Lord had promised him since 1952, that if he fulfilled some conditions, the Redeemed Christian Church of God would spread throughout the entire world. So the word of the preacher indicated that the conditions had been met.

On a certain day in the hotel, Pa Akindayomi called everyone together and announced Pastor Adeboye again as his successor. He did not end it there, he decided to do an impartation and transfer of mantle on him right in the hotel room. The prayers started and heaven sure came down. The fervent passion and power with which Pa Josiah Akindayomi prayed and laid hands on Adeboye caused an earth tremor in the area. Soon, the staff and management of the hotel felt the hotel was shaking physical like an earth quake was going to happen, they immediately sought help and it was traced to the room where an 'Elijah' was transferring his mantle to his 'Elisha'. The whole place shook, soon their room had to be inspected to check what kind of high powered machine they could be using. To the amazement of the hotel management, they realised there was no machine. There probably was no physical machine to point to but the potency of the prayer was sure high powered. This was the first point where Rev Josiah prayed for Pastor Adeboye as his successor transferring his mantle.

From that time on, Papa continued to take Adeboye through several series of prayers on their return. It is said that sometimes, Adeboye would come out drenched in sweat after both of them had been there praying, studying and transferring mantles for several countless hours.

UNDIVIDED LOVE FOR JESUS

On return, the Lord decided to test the extent to which Pastor Adeboye loved Him. Pastor Adeboye relays the test below,

"If you have to choose between Jesus Christ and your parents or your spouse, there would be no choice there because it has to be Jesus all the way. God may give you a test to find out whether you really mean to go with Him all the way. I loved my mum because I happened to be her only son and the last born. I was special. I can still remember vividly when I was sucking her breast. This will tell you how old I must have been at that time. There was no milk there but I was there because there was nobody to drive me away. There was this very strong attachment between my Mum and myself. I convened a Congress which was to take place at Ijebu-Igbo in December 1979 and because I knew that I would not be able to be with my Mum at Christmas, I decided to go and visit her a day before the programme. I drove home, got home late and the person who opened the door for me said it was God who brought me. She said my mother was dying. I went to her and she could hardly recognise me. I had to spend the night with her. Finally, she knew I was the one. We talked throughout the night. The programme was to start the following morning. It appeared that my mother was going to die on that day. I was now left with whether to go for the programme that I convened or wait and see my mother that I loved so much go away. When it was morning and I had to go, I told her that I loved her but I loved Jesus Christ more. I told her that I just had to go. It was like tearing my heart into two. However, it was a test. My mother did not die until 1990. In fact, as soon as I left she recovered. God just wanted to know whether I loved my Mum more than Him."

IF THEY CHOOSE TO GO, LET THEM GO

After the long announcements Pa Akindayomi had given his leaders for over two decades about Adeboye being his successor, the Lord told him to warn Adeboye that not everyone would support his leadership. According to Pastor Adeboye recalling the instruction, "A time will come when some will leave. Let them go for their leaving is for the good of the Church. Those who leave for whatever reason should not be taken back even if they wished to come back."

Pa Akindayomi also said they were in covenant to move the Church to the next level because the Redeemed Christian Church of God is a Covenant Church. The only requirement was that they both remain faithful to anything God required to bring the covenant to fruition. He said God had told him that the Church would spread far and wide all over the continents of the world. He said God had made a covenant with him that if one person leaves, a hundred would replace them.

True to the saying of Papa, when a close associate of Papa whom he knew might be a hard nut to chew for Adeboye heard of the choice of leadership, he left the Church. Not long after, he tried to come and beg Papa trying to come back but Pa Josiah did not take him back. He asked him to continue in his new found Church and that he had no grudges against him. God had already started clearing off obstacles one after the other, even before Papa left.

Pa Josiah was very clear as to his last instructions about Adeboye being his successor and he was careful to put all measures in place for it not to be altered. He went to the extent of making a tape recording of his last words which remained constant. He handed the tape to a trusted person in the presence of his wife. He warned that no one should try to alter the contents of the tape and if anyone did, such a one would have to bear the consequences of disobedience.

PAPA'S HOME CALL

Papa had told his members that one of his last assignments on earth would be to ordain a white man which he did in 1980. Hence, he was ready to go home since he had fulfilled all what God told him to do. Now the second quarter of 1980 came and very unlike Papa, he felt slightly ill with cough and body tiredness. As he grew weaker, he knew his time was close and he waited in anticipation to be called home. On the other hand, in September 1980, a prayer series was planned for him and people prayed in turns round the clock. He urged them to stop praying for his recovery because they were dragging back what had to be done. When the people were too zealous and they would not stop, he sent them out of his room and they prayed for him from another room.

By the middle of October, he gave up the ghost. Although, he came back to life to make some corrections, no one knew the exact duration of time for which he was dead but his wife also reported that she went in to his room and found him dead. While she was confused and about to break the news, he came back to life and related his experience while dead. He said he saw himself going along a fantastically beautiful path with a well laid garden; soon he met an old man who looked a bit familiar as though they had met before. The old man insisted that he had to go back to where he was coming from. He was so fascinated by the grandeur beauty of the place that he pleaded with the man to let him stay. The man declined and showed him exceedingly beautiful apparels which were hung ahead. The old man told him the apparels were for him (Pa Josiah Akindayomi) but he would not be able to claim it because he had not forgiven someone called Brother T. When he remembered that Brother T had offended him by burning his tract, he tried to explain to the old man but the old man insisted that the only option would be to go back and forgive Brother T. That was the moment he came

Pastor Adeboye teaching in his usual soft spoken but powerful style during one of the services at the 2008 Convention.

Pastor Adeboye holds one of the trophies awarded to outstanding provinces during the 2008 convention at the Redemption camp.

The 2008 convention was attended by well over 5 million people. A cross section of the multitudes of people raising their bottles of anointing oil as Pastor Adeboye ministers to them.

Hundreds responding to the altar call as Pastor Adeboye ministers, What an harvest of souls!

A cross section of over 5,000 Angelic Voices of the RCCG Mass Choir.

Popular Gospel Artist, Ron Kenoly totally overwhelmed with joy as he exchanges pleasantries with Pastor Adeboye after leading worship at the Redemption Camp, Lagos.

Pastor Adeboye and Pastor Benny Hinn shaking hands at the Redemption Camp, Lagos.

Bishop of Winners Chapel, David Oyedepo in warm greetings with Daddy and Mummy G.O.

Dr. Myles Munroe, Nassau, Bahamas congratulating Pastor Adeboye for his splendid contribution to the Body of Christ, at the RCCG Convention.

Pastor Ayo Oritsejafor, President of the Pentecostal Fellowship of Nigeria addressing the 5 million crowd in one of the Conventions of RCCG.

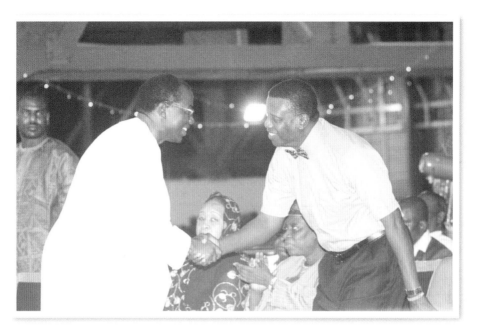

Governor Gbenga Daniels of Ogun State, Nigeria shaking hands with Pastor Adeboye while attending the annual RCCG convention.

Former Governor of Delta State, James ibori, saluting Pastor Adeboye having seen the massive crowds at the Congress.

What a connection! Big Daddy (God) giving Pastor Adeboye his son, specific instructions.

back to life again.

The Brother T being referred to was Pastor T Oshokoya, the leader of Apostolic Faith Church. The incident happened 28 years prior in 1952 when Rev Josiah saw a tract by Apostolic Faith Church, he liked it and since he couldn't write one, he decided to reprint it and use it for evangelism. As simple as it seemed to him being unschooled, he did not know he needed to have gotten the copyright owner's consent. He was called before the leaders of the Church and was found guilty. The rest of the tracts were retrieved from him and were instantly burnt right before his eyes. This act was amazing to him that his fellow Christian brethren would be so mean to burn up his tracts not considering the sacrifices he had suffered to afford the reprint of the tracts. Hence he held the grudge in his heart against the leader of the Church, Pastor T Oshokoya for the pains, loss and shame they put him through.

> " When you stand before the mirror of life, do you like what you see? "
> - Enoch Adeboye -

Without wasting time, as soon as he came back to life, he wrote to Pastor T Oshokoya telling him that he had forgiven him for the grudges he held in his heart against him for 28 years.

It was the set day, a beautiful Saturday; the final call was to be made. The day started beautifully as Papa received guests in his home who were returning from the foundation laying ceremony of a new branch in an area called Gbagada in Lagos. Many travelled down from Ibadan which is about 2 hours drive. As they told him how glorious the event was, he also spoke with them enthusiastically. Soon they left to their various abodes. Later, that evening Mrs. Folu Adeboye had travelled down from Ilorin where her husband was lecturing in the University. She told Pa Josiah she had to travel long hours down to Lagos to check his welfare since they kept getting rumours that his manner of speech was getting scary. Adeboye would have loved to make it there but he had just gone to check out his mother in another town called Ilesha.

Mama Akindayomi said the last statement her husband made to her that Saturday night when she entered the room was that everywhere there is a Redeemed Christian Church of God tomorrow, people will shout halleluyah. She couldn't make meaning out of the statement because she thought tomorrow was Sunday and it was normal for the people to shout halleluyah during the Church service. She did not understand that the tomorrow he meant was the future we see today.

Some three other Pastors named, Olonode, Solola and J.H.Abiona were in his room. They were to start all night prayers by 12 midnight. At about 11.30, when the prayers commenced, Mrs. Folu Adeboye and Mama Akindayomi were asked to stay in the living room. It was reported that one striking thing Papa did was that at several short intervals, he kept asking what the time was like someone with a set departure time for an air flight. He told Pastor Olukowajo the leader of the prayer team that he had also written the name of the person who would take over from him in a piece of paper hidden in his Bible, which he placed in his closet. When it was about 4.30am, i n the early hours of Sunday November 2nd 1980, he gave up the ghost and breathed his last.

> " Problems are revival pills to keep us spiritually healthy. "
>
> - Enoch Adeboye -

He was buried in the outfit he got from Israel. The particular Sunday morning was set as a day of thanksgiving for the whole Redeemed Christian Church of God branches instead of a day of mourning. These were his last request and it was followed to the letter. He was buried on the 6th of December 1980.

MY FATHER, MY FATHER

After Adeboye heard about the death of his Elijah, he was broken and he felt unworthy to step into the shoes but God encouraged him to be bold and courageous. The mantle definitely had finally fallen from an Elijah to his Elisha, from Pa Akindayomi to Pastor Adeboye.

Just like Pa Akindayomi told him that there would be oppositions about his assumption as the new leader God had chosen, he found it so. Many elderly and older Pastors felt insulted to be submitted to such a young man that even got converted right before their eyes. Some others had been there from the beginning and thought Adeboye was too inexperienced to lead them. These were the opinions of men but God had made His choice and only His counsel would definitely stand.

In the centre of the heat of oppositions, he was consecrated as the new leader of the Redeemed Christian Church of God in January 1981. He chose to be modest so instead of adopting the regular title of General Superintendent, he changed it to General Overseer and instead of his regular title of Reverend Doctor; he chose to be called Pastor. Pa Akindayomi's sealed pronouncement was finally read which made many leave to other Churches while some started their own Churches.

Quoting him in his recent days Adeboye said,

"The fact that I know how difficult it is to manage human beings, then again when you know that there were people... who started the Church in 1952, people who became Pastors before you became born-again, how do you say you want to become their boss? To me that would be stupid. But then, the foolishness of God is wiser than the wisdom of men. So when God decides, what can we do? It wasn't easy. I didn't want to be General Overseer. It was quite a struggle but as usual, He won. So when there were rumblings and shakings, God had already made it clear to me that the day I leave the Redeemed Christian Church of God, my first son will die. You see I'd rather take the beating than lose my first son. Your son is supposed to be the prime of your strength. So, it was tough, it was very challenging but I knew very well that this was not a job I applied for, knowing very well that this was not something I ever dreamt of becoming. I know the One that made the arrangement will see me through. Thank God that He has seen me through and I know that His grace will be sufficient for the rest of the journey."

Chapter

10

The Emergence Of The Glorious Church

Take a quick glimpse into the life of a young convert,
full of life and zeal, passionately rising to his colourful
destiny even in the fierce face of opposition and adversity.
Adeboye hung on to the promise of Christ that
He will build His Church upon the rock and the gates
of hell will not prevail. Soon, the Church of God
emerged in light and glory.

Chapter

10

*The Emergence
Of The
Glorious Church*

The phenomenal growth of the Redeemed Christian Church of God did not happen by sheer coincidence. This breakthrough growth was divinely orchestrated in heaven and was carefully placed as a seed in the heart of a visionary leader who strategically implemented God's vision with wisdom. Just as the emergence of Paul the First Century Church Apostle brought a wave of glory that changed the course of Christianity forever, the divine appointment of Pastor Enoch Adeboye as the General Overseer of the Redeemed Christian Church of God opened a new episode in the chronicles of the Church.

NOTHING JUST HAPPENS

All that had happened in his life prior to this defining moment in destiny had prepared him for the magnanimous task which lay ahead of him. Though a renowned University don, Pastor Enoch Adeboye did not rely on his academic prowess to conduct the affairs of the Church, rather like the King Solomon of old, he sought the face of the Lord in intensive and long seasons of fasting and prayers for divine blueprint for the new assignment. When he was ordained to lead the Church, he went into a retreat and he prayed for long days asking for the wisdom to go about it. Pastor Adeboye knew very well like he still knows today that the Church is the Body of Christ and belonged to Him alone and only Christ can grow His Church. Just as the Holy Writ says, "Except the Lord builds the house, they labour in vain that builds it". It does not matter how much efforts is put into the work of the ministry, if the Lord does not approve of it, it would not yield fruits.

DADDY, WHICH WAY TO GO

This strategy of first hearing from God is the deciding factor to every initiative Pastor Enoch Adeboye has introduced into the Redeemed Christian Church of God. Most of the initiatives that triggered massive growth in the Church and created global impact were birthed during seasons of intensive prayer, fasting and communion with his heavenly Father Whom he fondly refers to as Daddy. No matter how lofty any idea seemed, Pastor Adeboye would not approve of it without first enquiring from Daddy about it. When Pastor Enoch Adeboye became the General Overseer of the Redeemed Christian Church of God in 1981, the Church had about 40 parishes most of which were located in South-Western Nigeria. The vision which God gave Pastor Adeboye was to ensure that the Name of Christ is preached in Nigeria and beyond, through the Church. This necessitated the introduction of various Holy Ghost inspired initiatives and creative ideas aimed at making the Church grow in terms of membership, planting of more parishes and quality in the Christian life of members.

OPPOSITIONS TO CHANGE

During his long series of fasting and praying, he got so broken because he could see the glaring challenges he would have to face. At this point, he knew he would have to go into full time ministry work as a Pastor. He began to struggle within himself on how he would avoid financial constraints as a full time Pastor. When he remembered the humble background he grew from and the challenges of poverty he had to battle early in life, he was withdrawn from taking up the mantle of being the General Overseer. He began to weep for days until God consoled and reminded him that

" If your messages kill, a stake is reserved for you. If your messages heal, heavenly joy awaits you. "

- Enoch Adeboye -

all he achieved was by grace. The Holy Spirit comforted him and he was able to trust God in his step of faith. It was an awkward journey for him, but he yielded to the will of the heavenly Father. He did not allow even the dread of poverty to delude him from his vision.

FROM A MANSION TO A CUBICLE

After he had resolved to resign his opulent appointment at the University of Ilorin where he enjoyed the luxurious life of a senior lecturer, he remembered that he would be given his gratuity which he would use as a back up when confronted with the problem of sustaining his family in difficult times. His decision to accept the enormous responsibilities of the office of the General Overseer made it obvious that he had to also give up his house at the University which was a mansion. The boys-quarter at the back of his house was a two bedroom apartment and there was another guest lodge of two bedroom chalet attached to the house. It was an extreme sacrifice for Pastor Enoch Adeboye to give up all he had worked for and also his long time ambition of becoming the youngest Vice Chancellor in Africa.

Without any more contemplation, Pastor Adeboye knew he loved the Lord more than his comfort so he called his family together and intimated them about the decision to give up all they admired and follow the path of faith. Although the decision did not seem smart to leave his job in the University of Ilorin and move to Lagos to Pastor a group of mostly illiterates that resented him, however they all agreed since Pastor Adeboye was convinced that God was leading him. In a short while, they packed their belongings from the massive and comfy accommodation into a tiny one bedroom apartment in the house of the founder, Pa Josiah Akindayomi which was not even big enough to hold his books.

> " Obedience is an Island of treasures. Disobedience is an Island of torture. The boats to these destinations leave from the same harbour. Which one are you in? "
> - Enoch Adeboye -

FAITH HAS NO BACK UP

Although Pastor Adeboye had moved from his luxurious mansion in obedience to God, yet he had reserved his gratuity as a back up to help his family when the need arises. He applied for it and he was given. While preparing to save it, he heard God instruct him on how to spend the money. It was like God was in his business as he did not find peace saving the money. It was quite painful to give away his gratuity, his supposed last hope and reserve but he yielded to the voice of God. God instructed him to divide the money into three parts which he did. Then God showed him where to give the first part, then the second part and then the third. After he had obeyed, God told Pastor Adeboye to be totally dependent on Him as his only source.

The genuine heart of love for God and His work had consumed

Pastor Adeboye coupled with the strange encounters which he had with God. All these kept him going at such times when the goings were very tough. The Adeboye family had to sleep on a plank bed for more than eighteen months in that tiny one bedroom apartment in Mushin, Lagos. Soon God moved them to another level when a brother in the Church agreed to build a boy's-quarter for them on a plot of land beside the founder's house. They were excited and they celebrated this great miracle in love. The family moved into this apartment in 1983 and lived there for close to two years before they moved to Redemption Camp in 1985 according to the instruction of God. Pastor Enoch Adeboye dared all oppositions and consigned himself and his family to seasons of sacrifices when he had the option of keeping his well paying job as a senior lecturer at the University of Ilorin.

One phenomenon worthy of mention was the support and submission of his beloved wife Pastor Mrs. Foluke Adeboye. The sudden change of lifestyle from the very comfortable to the stringent life of poverty because of Christ could be a horrifying experience for any woman. She could have just left packing, but she stood her ground and continued to be of immense support in those moments of trials. She chose to follow the path of faith in God totally surrendering her will like a good example of the virtuous woman. What the Redeemed Christian Church of God is today is God's reward of that faithfulness, sacrifice and humility.

CHURCH CRISES

At that time, the Redeemed Christian Church of God with its small network of Churches was not without her own problems which were passed on to the shoulders of the new young and inexperienced General Overseer. But like the Biblical David, by the grace of God, he was able to defeat every giant on his way.

ADEBOYE IS NOT THE CHOSEN ONE

The number one problem was the mindset of many of the older Pastors in the Church, many of whom were already in the Church before him. They were not open to receive the change which the Lord was introducing into the Church through His servant; Pastor Enoch Adeboye. Many of them had earlier resented the fact that he was God's choice to take over from the Late General Superintendent. Some felt he had probably manoeuvred the old man by virtue of his education to make him his successor. This was not a big surprise to Pastor Adeboye because Pa Akindayomi had prophesied that there were going to be oppositions. Manoeuvring or manipulating the old prophet was totally fabricated because Pa Josiah made it clear the qualities, stature, and passion of the person who would succeed him long before he met Pastor Adeboye. So, the first time ever when Adeboye walked into the Church unsaved, Pa Josiah Akindayomi announced that the chosen one was among them and he went over to Enoch and Folu Adeboye's house after the service which had never happened. However, the more he tried to explain himself, the more rebellious the Pastors became, they chose not to co-operate with him or accept the things which the Lord was doing through him. Many of these Pastors left the Church to join another Church or start their own. Despite the hostile atmosphere in which Pastor Adeboye became the General Overseer some twenty-eight years ago, he decided to endure and remain focused.

GOD NOT EDUCATION, QUALIFIES

In addition to this, many of the older Pastors were uneasy about the fact that the new leader was a University Graduate with a Ph.D.

They wondered about what would happen to those who did not have even the secondary education and were already Pastors in the mission? They feared that they might lose their jobs. They developed a strong sense of insecurity and inadequacy. In the midst of the crises, Pastor Enoch Adeboye handled the issue with divine wisdom and assured the older Pastors in lengthy dialogue that his intentions were not to send anyone away on the grounds of educational qualifications. In order to tackle their problems, he extended warm hands of fellowship to everyone in the mission. To this end, the Bible College was established and it included courses in Yoruba language (local dialect) so that students could be taught in their native language.

> " If you can be bought at whatever price, you have lost your value. "
> - Enoch Adeboye -

LET'S BURY POVERTY WITH GIVING

Another major problem which confronted the young General Overseer was the issue of poverty. In those days, the total national tithe of the Church was N7, 000. By the time the Pastors, midwives and other Church staff excluding the General Overseer were paid, there was nothing left. The problem of poverty among the members then was serious. The people only gave tithes as there was no collection of offering of any sort. Pastor Adeboye sought the face of God when he remembered the challenges Pa Josiah had with finances before his glorious departure. He could remember an occasion when the Church needed N400 urgently for a project and the General Overseer and two of his most senior Pastors sat in his office for two hours racking their brains on how to get the money. Later, God miraculously intervened and sent a brother to give the General Overseer the money. Before that Divine provision, the men of God had considered the option of opening the tithe box before the due date.

This was how serious the problem of poverty was.

To overcome the problem, the Lord gave Pastor Enoch Adeboye a divine strategy. He began different teachings on Christian giving. As the Word of God began to take deep roots in the hearts of the people, they began to respond by giving to the work of the Lord. God also prospered the works of their hands. There were surprising interventions from God to the people as they obeyed. Many gave testimonies as they saw the faithfulness of God in their lives, businesses and finances. There was a positive turn on the tithes and this effected massive growth on the Church.

GOD LOVES CELEBRATION

At that time, the order of service was very monotonous. It was a solemn assembly which included only hymn singing, praise and worship and the likes. There were no drums and the use of musical instruments was not allowed. The sermons were very strict and centred only on holiness and the people engaged in much fervent prayers. However, the previous General Overseer had included in the constitution that the Church could introduce any new thing as long as it has its basis in the Bible. Amidst the struggles of a humble beginning, armed with the blueprint of the future and the power of the Holy Spirit, the new General Overseer commenced his work and began to prayerfully introduce new things in the Church. He introduced clapping and dancing unto the Lord and brought in the use of musical instruments to the praise of the Lord.

Recalling on those events, Pastor Enoch Adeboye later said,

"Once upon a time in our Church, guitar was forbidden, Drum? How can you drum in the house of God? One day I read Psalm 150 and thank God my father in the Lord told me when he was alive that the Bible is my constitution".

This new development met with great opposition from the conservatives within the Church, but as quality praise began to go up, blessings were coming down. And nobody questions results.

DIGGING DEEP, FAITH CLINIC AND HOME CELL

He introduced Digging Deep, a Bible Study weekly programme. It started as a small Bible Study group in the home of Pastor Enoch Adeboye but was later adopted as a Church program in the Redeemed Christian Church of God. This programme really helped to establish the members in the Word of God. The Church was exposed to the truth on diverse topics of the Bible. The programme was a huge success as it drew even non-members of the Church every Monday.

Then in 1982, Pastor Enoch Adeboye introduced another wonderful weekly programme called Faith Clinic; a healing prayer meeting. This programme was a platform where God began to demonstrate his power among the people and many people gave testimonies to the various miraculous signs in their lives. The Digging Deep and Faith Clinic effected growth on the Church to the glory of God.

> " Never ask God to give you the wealth you cannot control. What you cannot control will control you. What you cannot control, will dominate you. "
>
> - Enoch Adeboye -

In 1983, Pastor Enoch Adeboye travelled to South Korea and witnessed the operation of the Home Cell by Pastor Yonggi Cho. When he returned, he shared the idea with the Church and the house fellowship method was introduced the same year. This strategy has facilitated immense growth in the Church. Many of the Home Fellowship Centres became parishes of the Redeemed Christian Church of God.

MODEL PARISH

Among all the beautiful innovations which Pastor Enoch Adeboye began to effect in the Redeemed Christian Church of God, it was the Model Parish Movement that actually triggered the incredible pace at which the Church is moving today. Prior to the advent of the Model Parishes, the conservative mode of worship in the Church and its choice of location did not really appeal to some calibre of people in the society who were not in touch with the rather conventional scenery of the Church.

These people included young professionals, the learned and up-market individuals and captains of industries who felt out of place. Some of them were lecturers in the universities who loved Pastor Adeboye and were friends of the Church but refused to join because of the mode of worship. In the conventional setting, services tended to drag, and took longer time than many could contain. Then again the ascetic Pentecostal approach that was reminiscent of Puritanism and seemed legalistic as it tended to prescribe a dress code was definitely a turn-off to many.

The Model Parish Movement was to fill in this gap by creating conducive and better equipped worship environments where people from different walks of life would be able to worship the Lord in Spirit and in Truth without compromising the standard of the Word of God. The message remained the same but its presentation was adapted to appeal to the people in the upper sphere of the society, the likes of Nicodemus of the Bible.

When Pastor Adeboye first introduced the vision of the Model Parish, the conservatives within the Church opposed it. They misunderstood the vision completely and argued that it was a way of introducing worldliness into the Church. In May 1988, the first Model Parish of the Redeemed Christian Church of God was inaugurated. It was located at 1, Ladipo Oluwole Street, off Adeniyi Jones Ikeja with Pastor Tunde Bakare (now of Latter Rain Assembly) as the first Pastor.

The vision of the Model Parish Movement suffered a great deal of attacks that almost sniffed the life out of it but the grace of God sustained the vision. The second Model Parish was established in Ikoyi, Lagos at the St. Saviours Primary School, Alexander road, Ikoyi in August 1989. The third Model Parish was established in Apapa, Lagos on May 5, 1991 by Pastor Tony Rapu, a medical doctor.

Amidst all oppositions, and like a wildfire, different men and women of high calibre, doctors, bankers, engineers, lawyers, entrepreneurs, and the likes who would not ordinarily be attracted to the conventional method of presenting the Gospel began to find their way into the Church in their thousands. These people began to inject new zeal and vibrancy into the Church. Their approach to evangelism and Church planting was unparalleled. The Lord used the vision of the Model Parish to trigger massive growth in the Redeemed Christian Church of God. The Church grew from just 40 parishes which were only in South-Western Nigeria to over 25,000 parishes in more than 100 nations of the world.

THE GOD OF ALL CLASSES

Pastor Enoch Adeboye also introduced another wonderful initiative called Christ Redeemer's Friends Universal (CRFU). It was an initiative to evangelise the people at the very peak of the society like political and economic leaders, captains of industries, traditional rulers, and academia. The Lord through this strategy has brought many influential people into the Redeemed Christian Church of God.

Pastor Adeboye believes that there is nobody who is too high or too low to reach with the Gospel of our Lord Jesus Christ, the main issue lies in the method and strategy adopted. He is a man who believes in strategic evangelism. As the Lord continued to increase the Church and thousands began to flock in, Pastor Adeboye started the School of Disciples to train up men and women to militant Christians who would be empowered with the Spirit and knowledge of the word of God to destroy Satan's kingdom and possess nations for the Kingdom of God.

THE GOD FACTOR

The life of Pastor Enoch Adeboye has been totally enveloped in the "God-Factor". As a bond slave of Christ, he has totally surrendered his will to the Will of his Master. This reality is reflected in everything he does; even when he is on the pulpit preaching or praying for the millions of people that regularly converge to his several meetings. On the pulpit, it seems as if he does more listening to God than talking to the people. He would often say

> " If you let the gifts take over the place of the Giver in your heart, you will provoke God to jealousy and before long, He will demand for your Isaac. Be wise."
> - Enoch Adeboye -

something to the people, and then stay quiet for a few seconds turning his head sideways slightly as though hearing someone whisper the next thing to say into his ears. Then he breaks that small silence by saying, "Thank you Lord, Daddy said there is somebody here," then he gives an accurate word of prophecy concerning a person or a group of persons. Today, the evidence of a life of obedience to the instructions of God is reflected in the impact which the Redeemed Christian Church of God is making all over the world.

As he took up the mantle of leadership, he was careful to follow the directions of God. He did not care how unpopular or impossible those things which God instructed him appeared to the world, he chose not to veer off but stay focused. Being totally reliant on God helped him a great deal because the leaders, workers and members later saw the hand of God in the things he did and they joined him to celebrate the miracles that followed. That grace to hear distinctly from the Lord before taking any step was and still is one of the major secrets of Pastor Enoch Adeboye. Call it Divine Direction and you would still be right.

Looking at the glory and glamour which surrounds the office of the General Overseer of the Redeemed Christian Church of God today, one might be deceived to think that it had always been like that. Things had not always been as it is. The prosperity of today was conceived in the womb of poverty and lack. The millions of members we see today were birthed from very few who refused to quit when it was not easy.

Chapter

11

I Will Give You A City

Faith is a universal currency. When God promised Abraham an inheritance in the land of Canaan, he was a sojourner who had to pay for the plot of land where he buried Sarah his wife, he did not have any rights to the land. Against all odds, God fulfilled His promise and gave the entire land to him and his seed after him forever. Similarly, when God promised Enoch Adeboye that He will bless him with a city, the word came at one of the lowest moments in his life. He believed the word of the Lord and today, out of the shambles of a deserted forest, God has raised through him the largest Christian Estate in the world.

Your life can also be a reflection of the promise of God. If God has made you a promise to give you something, only patience, focus and faith will take you there. You can achieve that greatness in God. Nothing is impossible for God to give you, only believe.

Chapter

11

*I Will
Give You
A City*

REDEMPTION CITY, NIGERIA

After Pastor Adeboye assumed the leadership of the RCCG and had to vacate his opulent official quarters at the University of Ilorin where he was working as a senior lecturer, and relocate to a little one bedroom apartment of the General Superintendent at Mushin, a slum area of Lagos, it was a downturn experience for his family. Worried about the welfare of his family, Adeboye prayed to God asking Him to provide a more decent accommodation for his family. God assured him that He would not only provide for him a befitting accommodation, but would actually give him an entire city. Adeboye believed the Word from the Lord and when the congregation had grown to a few hundreds, he told them that the time was coming when the Church would be so large that the ministers would outnumber the present size of the congregation even ten times over. In 1983, the Lord instructed Pastor Adeboye to get a big land enough for a campsite for the Church He promised.

After much search, the Lord brought him to a thick jungle of forests located along the Lagos-Ibadan Expressway. At that time, the place was not habitable; it was rather a hideout for bandits and ritual killers. The forest was filled with many wild animals like snakes, scorpions, monkeys and gorillas. As thick as the forest was, Pastor Adeboye was convinced in his heart that it was the right place for them. He told his leaders that God had given them a land to possess and the mission purchased a little portion of the vast land.

After a while, Pastor Adeboye began to mobilize his members and they trusted God to build a 5,000 seated capacity auditorium. Some people thought that such a gigantic auditorium was too big and would only amount to waste of time and space because the entire congregation at that time was actually less than a thousand people. Pastor Adeboye had taken a glimpse into the near future and he knew that in a short time, the supposed big auditorium would be too small for the number of people that would gather at the camp. Volunteer work soon began on the land and with the help of the Lord the auditorium was completed as the first building to be constructed at the Redemption Camp. When the facilities at the Ebute-Meta Headquarters of the Church could no longer accommodate the crowd that attended the Holy Ghost service, the programme was moved to the Redemption Camp. That move brought the Camp to the public eye. After this, other buildings began to rise at the Camp. The office of the General Overseer was next to be constructed and Pastor Adeboye moved to the Camp as his workplace. In order to demonstrate his faith in the promise of God, he moved his family to the Camp in 1985 which was like a jungle without all the basic amenities such as electricity, water and good roads. The place was completely out of civilization. They remained there among the birds, animals with few of the locals being their neighbours. That was the beginning of the Redemption Camp which today has grown into a city and is arguably the largest Christian Estate in the world.

With time, the Church continued to acquire more lands in the area until it became really hard to say the exact size of the Redemption City. Other special functions of the Church were gradually moved to the Redemption Camp and along with the office of the General Overseer; some of the administrative offices of the Church were also moved to the Camp. Today, the Redemption City is the largest Private Estate in Nigeria and it spreads across two major States. It extends from the horizon of Shagamu in Ogun State to the borderlines of Ikorodu, the outskirt of Lagos.

> " When you have all your needs met and no enemy attacks you, not long after, when they tell you, Let us pray, you will ask, Pray to whom and for what? "
>
> - Enoch Adeboye -

The city has the following facilities;
An expansive and wonderfully laid out road network and drainage system.
A private supply of electricity,
A private clean water generating station
Many primary and secondary schools
A massive University with student hostels, staff quarters, laboratories, theatre, library and many more
Old Auditorium which seats over half a million people
Holy Ghost Arena, the seat of the world's largest auditorium
Banks,
Hospital,
All kinds of accommodation with Guest Houses of International standard
Private residences with thousands of houses, some of which are architectural masterpieces
Pastors Quarters
Many parishes of the Redeemed Christian Church of God
Orphanages
Police Station
The General Overseer Villa

The architectural design of the City was conceptualized by Pastor Enoch Adeboye. The story of the Redemption City attests to the fact that when God gives a promise to His anointed servants, He would make good His Word.

THE RCCG REDEMPTION CAMP, FLOYD, TEXAS

In a little over a decade, the Redeemed Christian Church of God in the United States has grown from just a handful of parishes into close to 400 parishes from Texas and Maryland to New York and North Carolina. Many years ago, the Lord revealed to Pastor Adeboye that the Headquarters of the RCCG in the US would be located in the State of Texas. At that time, there was not even one parish of the Church in Texas. God works in mysterious ways. A group of ministers of the Church were dining at a restaurant in Dallas one day, and then an American couple approached their table and said that God had instructed them to sell their landed property to the Church Group at the cost price. Prior to that time, God had instructed the couple to purchase the land many years back for a purpose which He would later disclose to them.

" When there is no challenge to keep you on your toes, you will become very complacent. When there is no more test, you cannot be promoted beyond your present level. "
- Enoch Adeboye

Before the purchase of the land, Pastor Adeboye inspected it and confirmed that it was a choice property for the Church to site her Headquarters in North America. That first purchase gave way to other properties within the parameters of that vicinity. As God would have it, the Church has continued to acquire more lands in that area. The Church is now building a multi-million dollar national Headquarters and conference centre in more than 600 acres of farmland in rural Floyd, Texas. The site is replicated after the Redemption City in outskirt of Lagos, Nigeria.

THE RCCG REDEMPTION CAMP, KENT, UNITED KINGDOM

The RCCG in the United Kingdom has been in the frontlines of Pentecostal movement in that country. The Church has been reputed as the fastest growing Christian denomination in Europe. Presently, the Church hosts the biannual festival of Life which is the largest Christian gathering in Europe with well over 60,000 people in attendance. Considering such magnanimous growth, the need for a Campsite where all the major events of the Church would hold is inevitable. The leadership of the Church in the UK set out on the mission to search for the landed property which would serve as the purpose. By Divine Providence, the leadership of the Church were introduced to the owners of a beautiful land at Chatham in Kent. The vast 146 acre land is located at the top of a scenic hill in Chatham. After series of negotiations the land was acquired for a giveaway price of One Million, Six Hundred Thousand Pounds. The title deed of the land was finally transferred to the name of the Redeemed Christian Church of God in February 2006. The Campsite would serve as the Headquarters of the RCCG in the United Kingdom and Ireland. Plans are underway for the site to be developed into a Retreat Centre with conference, exhibition and sports facilities. Also included in the master plan is the construction of chalets which would serve for retreats of individuals and groups. In near future, the major events of the Church would be moved from the Excel Centre to the Campsite.

Chapter

12

Church Without Walls

Paul the First Century Apostle, though not an eye witness of Jesus ministry received uncommon zeal and grace from the Holy Spirit and took the gospel to the darkest corners of the world where the other Apostles could not reach. Pastor Adeboye received a new vision of evangelising the whole world with the gospel of Christ. As you read on, you will discover how the Redeemed Christian Church of God received supernatural wings by the help of God and through the leadership of Enoch Adeboye to soar to over One hundred nations of the world. Daily, Churches are sprouting up like flowers and soon the beauty of God will spread through the earth.

Supposing you have a vision that looks too big to be accomplished, there is always a possibility in God. Your life, ministry, marriage, finance can be the envy of all. Get ready for supernatural explosions as you read this chapter.

Run and tell that young man with the measuring line that there are going to be so many people and so much livestock in Jerusalem that it will be too big to have walls (Zechariah 2:4).

HOLY GHOST SERVICE

In 1986, Pastor Enoch Adeboye repositioned the Church out of the confines of its building and practically took it to the highways and the byways when he started the monthly Holy Ghost Service. The emergence of this grand vision marked the wake of a new era in the history of the Redeemed Christian Church of God. Like all other divine initiatives which the General Overseer had implemented, the Holy Ghost Service was born out of his personal communion with God.

Pastor Enoch Adeboye was busy at his desk one day preparing the Church's Sunday School Manual when the voice of the Lord interrupted him with a question. "My son, what gift would you want for your birthday". At first, he was puzzled because since he got born again, he had not paid any attention to his birthday and he was amazed that God was interested in his birthday. He answered the

> " An understanding of the law of harvest makes you plan for your future. "
> - Enoch Adeboye -

Lord that he wanted each and everyone in his congregation to experience at least a miracle from the Lord to mark his birthday. The Lord then gave him the instruction to conduct a miracle service where the people would have an indelible encounter with Him.

In 1986 about 2,000 gathered for seven days at the Church Headquarters in Ebute-Meta for what was later described as Harvest of Miracles. The meeting was overwhelming as the power of God was present and many miracles were wrought. Each new day was more glorious than the previous. The following year, the facilities of the Church Headquarters was too small to accommodate the huge crowd which had come from different denominations, including non-Christians. The venue of the programme was moved to the Redemption Camp.

The Holy Ghost Service moved from being a yearly meeting to a monthly affair. As the months rolled into years, the Lord continued to enlarge the meeting and attendance grew larger. Then in 1994, the Lord took the Holy Ghost Service to unprecedented dimensions. For the first time, the Holy Ghost Service was held outside the Redemption Camp. The meeting was hosted at the Tafawa Balewa Square in Lagos, Nigeria in February 1994 with the theme: "The Battle of the Gods" with 67,000 people in attendance.

Also, in 1994, the Holy Ghost Service became an international event. The first international edition was conducted in London, United Kingdom and it was captioned 'The Festival of Life'. Today, 'The Festival of Life' has become a biannual event which holds at The Excel Arena in London and has been reported as the largest gathering of Christians in Europe with over 60,000 people in attendance.

The Holy Ghost Night took a transport-like shockwave to different cities in Nigeria. The service was conducted in Akure (October

1995), Port Harcourt (November 10, 1995), National Stadium, Lagos (December 1995), Kaduna (October 10, 1996), Ibadan (November 1997) and many more.

The violence and killings in higher institution of learning in Nigeria due to cult activities increased and youngsters were introduced to prostitution. Out of a fatherly heart of concern, Pastor Enoch Adeboye introduced Campus Holy Ghost Service to nullify these satanic operations in Nigeria's Tertiary Institutions. The first Campus Holy Ghost Service was held at Obafemi Awolowo University, Ile-Ife, in the year 2000. Other tertiary institutions such as Ogun State University, Ago Iwoye, University of Ibadan and University of Lagos have hosted the Campus Holy Ghost Service. During these meetings, thousands of students gave their hearts to the Lord and many renounced their membership of the cult.

It has also been hosted in many Nations of the world. In the United States of America, the Holy Ghost Service holds biannually at the Washington Metroplex and at the Redemption Camp in Dallas, Texas respectively. The Nation of Canada plays host to Holy Ghost Service yearly in the month of June. Other Nations that have had the opportunity to host the Holy Ghost Service includes Israel, South Africa, Germany, United Arab Emirates, Ghana and many more.

It has become a global platform where unprecedented crowds are drawn to worship the Father of light, souls are won into God's Kingdom and untold miracles, signs and wonders are performed by God in the lives of His children. Now, the Holy Ghost Service which holds monthly at the Redemption Camp, a suburb of Lagos, Nigeria has become the biggest regular and consistent gathering of human beings in the world

> " Disappointment, disgrace and shame are sisters of over-confidence. They always flock together. Disown over-confidence today! . "
>
> - Enoch Adeboye -

with attendance in millions. The Lord has kept His covenant with His servant. This monthly meeting has continued to be an arena where the miracles of God happen continuously.

LEKKI '98

Sometimes in 1998 while Pastor Adeboye was returning from a trip to the USA, he drove across Lekki Beach in Lagos in company of some of his children in the Lord. He thought of how Christ would gather the multitudes by the seaside and teach them the Word of life with healing, signs and wonders. At that instant, the Holy Spirit dropped in his heart the gigantic vision of hosting four million souls in one meeting for the purpose of worshipping the King of Kings; Jesus Christ, to experience the mighty move of God for healing, signs and wonders in unprecedented dimensions and the salvation of the souls of many.

> " The sacrifice you make and price you pay will determine the size of your container for the anointing you will receive. "
> - Enoch Adeboye -

To the glory of God, that same year Pastor Adeboye led the Redeemed Christian Church of God to host what was described by international observers as the largest gathering of human beings up till that time. The event which held under the open skies at the Lekki Beach on December 18, 1998 was captioned Divine Visitation. The crowds were there in excess of the expected four million people. It attracted the International Media and CNN. With an aerial view, they estimated that the crowd could not be less than over six and a half million people attending the event.

The city of Lagos stood still on the glorious night of the Lekki '98 crusade. People came by air, road and sea. One of the amazing things was that despite the people that walked for miles, others that came by air and those on their boats, there was no record of deaths or loss of life. It was a sea of humanity. The shouts of hallelujah from this mammoth crowd electrified the air and quaked with a vibration that could be heard many miles away. The people worshipped the Lord and there was indeed a Divine Visitation. At a point, it seemed as if hosts of angels had mingled with the crowd as miracles began to take place from all quarters.

Many lame people began to abandon their wheelchairs as the power of the Lord swept through the crowd. The blind received their sights and diverse miracles happened to the glory of God. There were tens of thousands of people who had come out to give testimonies to the miracles of God in their lives and there was very limited time in the all night event. Only eternity can fully comprehend the impact of the programme on the lives of those who attended from every corner of the world. When the altar call was made for salvation in Lekki '98, people had to trek almost one kilometre to the altar.

The event was also given a live broadcast by all the major television stations in Nigeria. There were more millions of people that were part of the service in their homes through the live broadcast than those who were at the venue of the programme. It was indeed an unforgettable experience. Lekki '98 is evidence that there is no vision that is too insurmountable to achieve for God.

The following year the venue was shifted to the Redemption Camp where the second edition was held in 1999. It was a 3 day event with the theme: Victory at Last. The third one was also held at the Redemption Camp in 2000 with the theme Open Heavens. In the year 2001, Pastor Adeboye christened this annual special event as Holy Ghost Congress and moved it to a specially constructed Arena at the Redemption Camp.

HOLY GHOST CONGRESS

In the third week of December of every year, the city of Lagos play hosts to the master of all events. This event is larger than the world cup, the Olympics, any show or carnival anywhere in the world. Each year, the Holy Ghost Congress attracts over seven million people from over 30 different Nations and from all the Continents of the world. They come to the Redemption Camp for one purpose; to worship Jesus Christ the King of kings and the Lord of lords. The Holy Ghost Congress is the largest gathering of human beings in history. It is amazing that such a history making event is happening on our planet and the world knows only little about it. The Congress is absolutely the most under-reported global event.

The congress which holds for six days is a magnificent mind-blowing sea of humanity. There is absolutely no words that can compare, it is better seen and experienced to comprehend. There is an overwhelming feeling that floods the atmosphere as Seven Million people raise up their hands to worship and elevate Jesus Christ. The atmosphere literally gets charged, one can actually feel the current of the power of God in the air. It is like an earthquake when with one voice all the people make a resounding shout of Hallelujah. The people get raptured into an ecstatic spirit-filled worship. Another incredible feature of the Holy Ghost Congress is the array of healing, miracles and wonders which earmark the event as the place where the Lord God visits his people. Countless miracles of the lame walking, the blind seeing, healing of cancer, tumour, HIV, and even creative miracles of short legs growing back to normal are commonplace at the Holy Ghost Congress.

The six days of the Congress is an array of various events such as teachings, seminars, workshops, special anointing services, special healing programs, children and youth meetings. Each of the programmes focuses on wholeness of the total man with emphasis on the salvation of the soul, health for the body and God's empowerment in the spirit.

Many souls are won for Christ in the course of the six day event. Many Church Leaders, Gospel Artistes from different nations and denominations always attend the Congress to minister to the people; it is always power packed. Many prominent men and women of God from around the world have visited the Holy Ghost Congress and testified to the fact that it is the largest gathering in the world. Bishop T.D. Jakes, Pastor Benny Hinn, Pastor John Hagee, Pastor Ted Haggard to mention a few, have all witnessed the power of God at the Holy Ghost Congress. In 2003, visiting American Guest Pastor, Jerry Hobbs was overwhelmed by the mammoth crowd and made the following remarks, "I have often wondered at Moses leading the millions of the children of Israel at Red Sea into Canaan, coming to the Holy Ghost Congress, I can well imagine what it was like". International media such as the BBC (British Broadcasting Corporation), CNN (Cable Network News), and CBN (Christian Broadcasting Network) have covered the Congress at one time or the other.

The climax of the congress is the all night miracle service of Friday which extends to the early hours of Saturday, which is the last day of the annual event. Pastor Adeboye leads the people in a nonstop twelve hour service of various sessions. There is time of intensive praise and worship led by a 5000 mass choir. There are many people who have come from different nations, but everyone present has one need; to receive the tangible and indelible touch of Jesus. Every heart is broken and expectant of a miracle from God.

The prophet of God for our time, Pastor Enoch Adeboye steps on an altar as large as the size of a football stadium shortly after the choir offers a rendition, which is proceeded by the play of saxophone by Pastor Kunle Ajayi, his personal minstrel. In his usual solemn but penetrating tone, Pastor Adeboye breaks the few seconds of silence with a resounding "Let Somebody Shout Hallelujah". Then Daddy G. O. as fondly called would begin to declare to the people the things which the Lord had assured him to do for His people for that night. There is thunderous noise of clapping and shouting as the elated crowd who knows very well and have witnessed the fact that when the God of Adeboye says something, He would do it.

As the teachings and prayers continue, the healing and miracles begin to take place and shouts of joy begin to echo from different quarters of the behemoth size auditorium. It is an unimaginable experience. At this point, the testimonies begin to flock in but they are too many to count. Everyone who attends the Congress always goes back home with a testimony to the power of God in their lives. It is difficult for anybody to comprehend the enormity of this heaven on earth annual event except by a firsthand experience. Every assiduous seeker of God all over the world should mark their calendar for the next Holy Ghost Congress by the third week of December every year. There is no better place to be.

The administration of the event is another thing that is worthy of mention. For the entire six days, everything is masterfully co-ordinated. The food, accommodation, transportation and other logistics is all well done. A detail of some statistics at the 2006 Holy Ghost Congress might be able to give a glimpse into the magnificence of the event. The meeting is hosted in what is the largest auditorium in the world ever. It is an incredible, overwhelming seven miles behemoth. Fully assembled, the construction materials alone would require no less than five ocean going vessels to convey.

Attendance: 7.4 Million people
Registered Ministers: 40,000
Ushers: 5,000
Counsellors: 4,000
Choir: 2,500 voices
First Aid Centres : 30
Sanitation Squad : 4,000
Prayer Intercessors: 10,000
Hundreds of Commuter Buses
Guest Ministers from 30 Nations and the six continents
A football stadium size main altar supported by 84 mini altars
Taxis and Motorcycles to transport people to and fro the magnani-

mous arena.

MEDIA MINISTRY - REDEMPTION HOUR

Over two decades ago, televangelism was not very popular in Nigeria. Very few ministries use the power of the media to broadcast the message of the Gospel. Pastor Enoch Adeboye was one of the pioneers of televangelism in Africa. He was convinced that the television was a powerful avenue to spread the Word of God and the activities of the RCCG to those people who might not walk into the walls of a Church building.

> " Check all the excesses of comfort in your life and take steps to have mastery over whatever God gives you. "
> - Enoch Adeboye -

Adeboye made a call for members of the Church who were professionals in electronic media to form a team that would effectively run the television ministry of the RCCG. Pastor Syngle Wigwe retired Director General of the Nigerian Television Authority; the largest TV network in Africa became the pioneer director of this ministry. After the launch of the media ministry of the RCCG, they began to broadcast the teachings of Pastor Adeboye and the special events of the Church on the platform of The Redemption Hour. Today, the Redemption Hour broadcasts on many television stations across Nigeria.

DOVE MEDIA GROUP

With the advent of the satellite broadcasting, Pastor Adeboye saw the need for the Church to extend the media outreach to all the nations of the world through satellite television. The media ministry of the RCCG birthed the Dove Media. The new initiative had the objective to operate a global satellite television, radio, internet, multi-media studio and prints. The dove media went through some rough moments but eventually stabilised its operatives. Presently, the Dove Media under a new management headed by Patrick Abraham from the arm of the group in the UK has launched a twenty-four hour satellite television on two channels;

> " The heat and barrage of attacks you are going through are evidence of your enemies' fears. No matter how weak you think you are, you are stronger than them. "
> - Enoch Adeboye -

Disc Communication, a cable pay TV and HiTV. Work is on to add two additional channels in Johannesburg, South Africa and Accra, Ghana. Dove Media also broadcast via Internet Protocol Television at www.rccgdovelive.org. The Dove Media also broadcast the Gospel through the Internet Radio. The Dove Media has also produced many Gospel movies.

The Media House has effectively and consistently produced live broadcasts on the monthly Holy Ghost Night and the Holy Ghost Congress. In 2009, the 57th annual convention of the Church marked a milestone for the Dove Media. During the entire period of the convention, signals were transmitted live via five television networks; Disc Communication, HiTV, GTV, MyTV Africa, View Africa Network, and on the Dove Media IPTV at www.rccgdovelive.org to millions of viewers in different parts of the world.

With headquarters in Lagos, Nigeria the Dove Media has branches in the UK and the United States. It has a hi-tech digital studio that is equipped with state of the art equipment. The Dove Media has continuously invested heavily in the production of televangelism, wireless internet link service, video musical productions and promotions of Gospel music in Africa.

OHTV (OPEN HEAVEN TELEVISION)

Apart from the Dove Media, Pastor Adeboye has launched another 24 hour satellite television broadcasting from the United Kingdom on Skye Channel 199 called the OHTV. This Christian channel broadcasts contemporary Christian programmes, music, movies and shows targeted at the young people. The OHTV reaches a potential viewership of 2 million people.

PUBLICATIONS OF OVER 150 TITLES

Pastor Adeboye has used the printed pages to spread the Gospel of Jesus Christ more than anyone else on the continent of Africa. He is an accomplished author of over 150 titles with more being constantly published. His books cover extensively on all subjects of life from Christian living, family life, leadership, divine prosperity, singleness, youthfulness, sacrifice, discipline, divine direction, favour, open heaven, divine visitation, motivation and many more. His books have been translated in many languages and have sold in tens of millions all over the world.

POWER, PRAISE AND PURITY DEVOTIONAL BIBLE

In 2001, Pastor Adeboye released the Power, Praise and Purity devotional Bible. It was the first time an African would publish a commentary Bible. In this classic work, Adeboye shared from his wealth of knowledge and experience to empower the next generation of Christian leaders towards the three most essential secrets of a successful Christian life and ministry; purity, praise and power. The PPP Bible sold numerous copies and became a huge blessing to the

Body of Christ all over the world.

OPEN HEAVEN DAILY DEVOTIONAL AND E-OPEN HEAVEN COMPENDIUM

In 2001, Pastor Adeboye released the Open Heaven Daily Devotional, another powerful tool to disciple and to empower Christians. In 365 days, Pastor Adeboye helps the reader to begin the day on a positive note by sharing on different subjects for each day. The devotional also has other features such as 365 day Bible reading plan, practical action plan, special prayers, thought for the day and memory verse. The devotional has helped many Christians in their faith walk and has challenged them towards the fulfilment of their divine destiny. It is produced in different languages and distributed globally. In 2008, the Open Heaven Daily Devotional was produced in a digital form called the e-open heaven compendium. Branded as a software, the digital project has special features such as 4 years of Open Heaven Devotional with Audio Reading, Complete KJV Bible with Audio Compatibilities, Hebrew and Greek Bible with Audio Compatibilities, Exhaustive English and Strong's Concordance, Search Engine, the PPP Bible Commentaries, Gospel Hymns, Bible Reading Plan and many others. This project is the first of its kind in Africa.

> " Increasing by labour is good. Increasing by favour is far better. Which one do you choose? "
>
> - Enoch Adeboye -

INTERNET

As a Christian organisation, The Redeemed Christian Church of God has one of the largest web presence on the Internet. It has tons of websites hosted by different parishes and ministries from all over the world. There are countless articles, blogs and twitter pages carrying one information or the other about the Church.

Adeboye in his usual humble self always makes conscious efforts to exalt the Name of Jesus Christ, to promote the cause of the Redeemed Christian Church of God and while at it, to remain silent about blowing his own horns. However, Pastor Adeboye has distinguished himself as a vessel unto honour in the Hands of God and has used every available tool and avenue to spread the Gospel of Jesus Christ to the far ends of the earth.

Chapter

13

I Am Serving A
God Of Miracles

There are no special seasons for miracles but there is a special God of miracles. The simple command of Jesus Christ to every believer to heal the sick, cast out devils, cleanse the lepers and raise the dead is still relevant to the Twenty First Century Christian. God's servant, Pastor Adeboye takes God's word for healing and special miracles as literal as it is said in the Bible. With faith, he ministers to many sick, afflicted and oppressed every passing month and the power of God is revealed.

Do you have a sick loved one? Have you been diagnosed with a terminal ailment? Did you get a heart breaking doctor's report? Do not be frightened! There is a great healing power of Christ available as you read and flip through the pages of this book. You can receive that long awaited healing now! You can overcome that ugly situation by the words of the testimonies in this book. Hang on friend, say a word of prayer and watch the miracle worker, Jesus, at work again.

Chapter

13

*I Am
Serving
A God Of
Miracles*

I AM SERVING A GOD OF MIRACLES

If we were to write the testimonies that are recorded in one year's crusade of Pastor Adeboye, it will surpass the entire volume of this book. Salvation of thousands of souls every month is recorded as people rush out to give their lives to Jesus and take a new turn.

There are countless creative miracles that are being reported daily in the ministry of Pastor Enoch Adeboye, some of which are here, that surpass human reasoning. He is a man of faith that believes the Word of God literarily. He has seen the various interventions of God at different instances in his life which makes his life challenging to the ordinary man. Many people always go back to hospitals disdaining their doctors with the miracles that happen. Imagine the testimony of people who receive divine healing from such terminal diseases like HIV/AIDS after contact with clothes that were blessed by Pastor Adeboye during a crusade. There is no human logic that can grasp the testimony of a baby living in the womb without a placenta for 8months, one lung turning to two or the incredible growth of imperfect body parts, goitre disappearing, sanity restoration, paralysed walking, curing hypertension, fibroid disappearing, curing of liver problems, financial freedom, return of long lost family members, cancellation of debts, change of genotype, healing of strokes, restoration of sight to the blind, leukaemia disappearing, examination success, deliverance of the captives and fruitfulness to the barren are regular in the meetings Pastor Adeboye conducts. He is one humble man with a big God working in his favour.

MY FIRST HEALING

The first time this great healing evangelist experienced personal healing was when he was struck with fever and could not go for Bible Study. He was lying on his bed totally down but God's hand reached him there in his home. He took a step of faith and decided to have his own Bible study at home. He put in a preacher's tape to listen to. It seemed everything the preacher said pertained to him. Suddenly the preacher began to quote the Bible in I Peter 2:24 that by the stripes of Jesus, we were healed. He then said, if we were already healed, no one should allow sickness in their body. Enoch believed what he heard immediately, he began to feel uncomfortable where he slept. He suddenly jumped up, stopped the tape and rushed to Church. When he got to Church, the teacher taking the Bible Study said everyone should jump up and dance. He wondered how he would be able to do that because he was so sick and tired that he felt like falling over. Soon, he mustered up little strength to get up holding on to the pew. Then, he felt like urinating, he went to the toilet and came out well and healthy. God had healed him completely. That was the first time ever he experienced the supernatural healing power of Jesus in his life. Little did he know that God was going to use him mightily to heal others.

YOU HAVE THE POWER TO HEAL

Pastor Adeboye, who had experienced the healing power of God in his life has ministered the same miracles to those in need all around the world. This is one of his testimonies on his encounter of the power of God as a young minister.

"I was in Ilorin and for six months I cried to God to give me power. That was my only prayer at that time. One night, God spoke to me and asked me what I had done with the power He had already given me. I told him that if I had power I would not be asking for it. He asked if I had been baptized in the Holy Spirit and I answered in the positive. He asked me to quote what was written in Acts 1:8 and I said, 'Ye shall receive power after the Holy Ghost is come upon you'. He asked whether I had tried to use the power or not. I promised to lay hands on the next sick fellow I met. On the following morning, one of my members brought somebody whose child was sick and had not slept for two weeks. Doctors could not help. They said that the child would die. The member brought the mother and the sick child to me boasting that if I prayed for the child all would be well. I wondered why she could not pray for the child herself. I was worried and God reminded me of my decision that I would lay hands on the next sick fellow brought to me. I said that the decision was made in the night when it was dark and I was alone. There was nowhere to run to so I picked up the child and I prayed. As I was praying, the child went limp and I thought the child had died. When I opened my eyes I noticed that the child was fast asleep. That was the end of the sickness."

This was the beginning of great things in the healing ministry of

> " Anyone who does not contribute to your progress in any way is an excess luggage: drop the fellow. "
>
> - Enoch Adeboye -

Pastor Adeboye. Here are some testimonies.

3 DEAD RESTORED TO LIFE

Mr and Mrs Akpavie were on their way to the Friday Holy Ghost Congress with their 3 kids and a nephew. Suddenly strange things started to happen to them, one of their children started to make strange sounds that got the couple startled, before they could reason out what was happening, the child began to foam. In the heat of that torture, the other two kids began to make the same strange sound. They pulled over the car to one side and started to scream. In splits of minutes, the 3 children had foamed and were cold dead. Even the visiting nephew too started getting cold.

" If you cannot identify the appropriate key, you will be barred from entering your breakthrough. "
- Enoch Adeboye -

When they got too scared, they beckoned on passing cars that were going to the same meeting. The people stopped and there began a crusade as they laid the dead children on the streets. Everyone began to pray and call on the God of Elijah and Adeboye to raise the dead children and revive the fourth child to normalcy. Right in the middle of the road, God heard their cry as they prayed, the kids were instantly brought back to life and fully revived.

11 YEARS BARREN WOMAN GIVES BIRTH TO TRIPLETS

There was a woman who had been barren for 11 years, she was already in a frustrated state when God showed up for her. After about the first 5 years of waiting on God for a baby, she began a hospital tour, as she moved from one doctor to the other seeking for solution to her problem. The doctors could not find any concrete reason for her lack of conception. Two more years passed and she was 7 years barren when she was given the sudden news that she had conceived. In the euphoria of the long awaited joy, Satan struck and she lost the pregnancy she waited seven years for. She became bitter and deeply agonised against her unfortunate condition. When the shame became unbearable after 9 years of waiting and no solution, she decided to commit suicide but God stepped in.

Soon, she was invited to go on a trip to Israel with Pastor Adeboye, which she did. When they got to Solomon's temple, Pastor Adeboye told everyone to write their request and put it on the wall. In her request, she prayed that God will bless awaiting couples with children and that particularly, she wants to be blessed with a triplet as a compensation for her years of waiting. Amazingly, few months after the trip, she conceived. Eventually she gave birth to a set of triplets without any complications, after 11 years of barrenness.

FEATHERS DISAPPEARS FROM WOMAN'S ARMPIT

In one of the crusades, the Lord gave a very strange word to Pastor Adeboye of a woman who had feathers in her armpits instead of hair. When he heard the word, he was surprised because he had never seen such a situation all his life but he quickly said the word of knowledge not really expecting anyone to come out. Alas, a responsible woman came walking out indicating that was her problem. Daddy G. O as fondly called, prayed for her and she was totally delivered. Here is Pastor Adeboye's words recapping the incident,

"We went to hold a Holy Ghost Night at the Liberty Stadium. The stadium was full, inside and outside. I was just rounding up to go when suddenly God spoke to me and said that there was a woman in the crowd with feathers in her armpits instead of hairs. The Lord said I should call her out because He wanted to solve the problem. I was reluctant to call her out because I thought she will not come out. So, I made the announcement, I thought nobody would come but the woman came and I thought, probably, she did not understand what I said. I explained again. She said she was the one. We prayed a simple prayer and the Almighty God took away all her problems."

CANCER VANISHES

This particular woman was diagnosed of Cancer. She was a patient of various hospitals including University Teaching Hospital Ibadan, Sacred Hospital, Ikeja Hospital and General Hospital Lagos. When the cancer became critical, she would slump in the public. In the midst of it, she received 3 letters from Pastor Adeboye encouraging her and he also prayed for her. It looked like the cancer was getting worse as she had spent all her money on chemotherapy. Soon, she became bed-ridden because she could hardly walk. She testified that at the time, she had swellings all over her body and her liver was inflamed. She even got so skinny that even the doctors avoided seeing her. She was left to counting days to her grave.
She was brought to the Holy Ghost Service in November 2007, the Word of Knowledge came from Pastor Adeboye that God had healed her liver and that the rest of the sickness in her body would vapour away within the next 3 months. According to the word of God from Pastor Adeboye, she was miraculously healed.

MOSLEM MAN SAVED FROM DEATH

Mr Habib, born Moslem but married to a Christian was reluctantly persuaded to attend the Holy Ghost meeting with his wife for the first time. He concentrated on the word of God that was being preached by Pastor Adeboye and he felt the power of God touch him. Pastor Adeboye gave a word that the clothes that everyone wore were being anointed by God and that they should wear it to important occasions and places they needed to go.

> " The extent of your fear of God is the extent of hatred you have towards sin. "
> - Enoch Adeboye -

On a particular day, he was in a car with his wife and another minister from the Church. Suddenly they realised a fuel tanker had collapsed on the way and it was about to explode. His wife and the minister succeeded in escaping the scene before the explosion but Mr Habib was caught up in the fire. As he began to run with fire all over his clothes which Pastor Adeboye had prophesied over, he kept shouting Holy Ghost Fire. He was immediately rushed to the hospital (Lagos University Teaching Hospital) where he was taken care of. Miraculously, he sustained only minor injuries because of the anointed clothes he was wearing and was discharged while the other 29 people that were in the same fire all died.

25 YEARS OF ASTHMA DISAPPEARS

There are usual records of God healing asthmatic patients. Hence, the case of the man named Adigun is worthy of note. Although the ailment started 25 years ago with sneezing, catarrh and cough, so much that Adigun could not stay in any air-conditioned room, nor could he use cold water to bathe or drink. He was first diagnosed and treated for pneumonia, as the sickness persisted; he was later diagnosed with Chronic Asthma.

From then on, he would have attacks in public places and would be rushed to the hospital. He was often given several injections and medication that only gave temporary relief. He was told that he would have to live with Asthma for the rest of his life. Incidentally,

Pastor Adeboye was invited to preach in the Abuja branch of the Redeemed Christian Church of God. He happened to be in the meeting so Pastor Adeboye laid hands on him. He came for the subsequent meetings and the Word of Knowledge was released in his favour. To God's glory, ever since then, the Chronic Asthma condition has disappeared and he has been living in divine health.

GENITAL PAIN DISAPPEARS

A particular man came for the Holy Communion service in October 2007. He had been sick with pain in his private area. It started like a casual discomfort but not much attention was given to. After two years the pain had become unbearable. He went to the General Hospital to see a physician, he was given several medicines which he used but it was all to no avail. He was referred to a Specialist and Consultant at the Federal Medical Centre, who told him he would have to do a surgery which will affect his potency. Getting this news made him sad and he was left with the option of living with it for the rest of his life. In serious pain, he decided to attend the Holy Communion meeting at the camp. After partaking of the communion, he was made perfectly whole according to the word of God's servant on that day.

MAN WITH THE ISSUE OF BLOOD

A gentleman named Andrew was healed by the power of God during the Holy Ghost Congress. He had a disease which the doctors could not classify. Anytime he went to urinate, he would pass out blood instead. He had visited countless hospitals, seen several doctors till all hope was lost. When he was given medication for relief, it would escalate the condition, resulting to reactions such as his tongue sticking out and twisting simultaneously. His issue of blood continued for over 25years until the Friday when he was in the crusade.

As Pastor Adeboye was ministering, he paused as usual and said 'Daddy said (referring to God) there is someone here who is urinating blood, you can go and check now, it has stopped.' Andrew could not believe what he heard, he sat startled till the end of the meeting that day. Getting back to the room he lodged in the early hours of the Saturday morning, he went to check himself in the toilet and to his greatest amazement, the blood had ceased from his urine. From that day, he has been living hail and hearty.

> " The quality of your service determines whether you will be easily replaced or not. "
>
> - Enoch Adeboye -

BLIND BOY RECEIVES SIGHT

It was in one of the early ministry days of Pastor Adeboye when he used to conduct the Congress in different States of Nigeria that this healing of a blind boy took place. Pastor Adeboye recalls the event, "Several years ago, we were having a programme that we called Congress. We used to have it in several places at the same time. At that particular year we had it in three places, Otukpo, Sapele and Akure and I was travelling with a team, visiting the various centres. In Sapele while preaching, God opened my eyes and I saw a vision in which I saw a young boy that was born blind, whose eyes suddenly opened. So I shouted, 'There is a boy here whose eyes God wants to open. If you are the father or the parents, bring the boy forward.' Nobody moved. I knew what I saw. I said, 'or if the boy is at home, go and bring him I will wait'. I waited and waited but nobody came.

Sadly, we left for Akure. I was sad because I knew that I saw a miracle happen. Anyway, we got to Akure and somebody else was preaching. I was at the back of the auditorium. All of a sudden, while the preaching was going on, I saw a man stand up, holding a boy. It was the boy that I saw in the vision. The man was leading the boy towards the altar and I knew that the ushers would not allow them to get near the altar at all. Hence, I began to run to try to tell the ushers to let them pass. As I was running, the boy heard footsteps behind him and turned and as he turned, his eyes opened. "

OCCULT MAN TURNS TO JESUS

In the ministry of Pastor Adeboye, there have been countless occult members and diabolic people who have dropped their charms and made their ways to the cross. This was the case of one Mr Tunde that met with Jesus like Saul of Tarsus did. This said man was born into the occult and grew up in the midst of rituals. When he became of age, he followed the path of his predecessors and became an Herbalist. He was the Asipa Ogboni (Leader of an Occult Fraternity) and Coordinator of Odua Peoples Congress (A Militant Group). These are groups that are fanatical in diabolic and fetish worship. They claim to be the ones that empower many rulers and support many atrocities in the Nation. The people in this group are usually empowered and immune to gun shots using Black Magic.

This particular man reported that he usually did not need to enter a car or any other means of transportation to travel for distances in excess of 50miles. He could disappear from city to city, town to town with the charms he used.

In September 2007, on his way to a particular meeting from Oyo state to Ogun state (about 120 miles). He recited his usual incantation and was ready to take off when he realised his charms took him to a wrong destination. He buckled up and was ready to reschedule his invisible journey back to his initial destination. As he was about to take off, he saw 3 men in front of him wearing white apparels, he also noticed they held Bibles in their hands. The one in the middle was very tall, he held his hands and told him that his voodoo power had become impotent because he will be clothed with a power that is above the charm. He was shocked as he stood pondering when the men directed him to a Church and left his sight. Discarding what he saw and heard, he continued to say his incantations ready for his usual flight when he realised the charm was working wrongly. Instead of taking off, he began to experience a burning sensation that made him act abnormal in the presence of people in the area. He felt so uncomfortable and ran to the Church which happened to be a Parish of the Redeemed Christian Church of God, they had pointed to him. On getting there, the people were frightened because they saw all the charms he had on him. He relayed his story and they preached to him and burned his charm. He was not allowed to sleep in the branch of the Redeemed Church of God he ran to, so they took him to Redemption City for more prayers, and he was clothed and fed. Ever since, the delivering power of God has been working in him as he vomited other charms he had swallowed. Till date, he has remained a follower of Jesus Christ, exposing the works of the devil and saving others.

MIRACLES AT THE MATERNITY CENTRE

Sis Funmi got married in year 2000. Shortly after, she took in and was expecting her baby. After the normal months of waiting, she went to the hospital and was told to come the next morning to be delivered of her child. Shockingly, when she got to the hospital the next morning, the doctor said the child in her womb had died. Although she had contractions, the baby was to be brought out dead. They tried all they could for her to be delivered but it was all to no avail. She moved from one hospital to the other seeking for help. She was slated for an operation 5days later but she was delivered of the dead child miraculously 30minutes to the set time for the operation. She was discharged and sent home with tears.

Shortly after, a month later, she conceived again and when it was delivery time, the baby's hand was fractured by the midwives. From 2 weeks old, the child had to be regular at the Orthopaedic Hospital, Igbobi for treatments. After series of treatments, fasting and prayers, the baby's hands were restored and okay.

" To be successful in any area of life, it is good to study the lives of others who had succeeded in that particular area, to find out what they did which other people ignored. "
- Enoch Adeboye -

When this baby became 3 years old, Sis Funmi conceived again. After nine months, she went to the Hospital again to be delivered of the child on the set day. The baby was out at the time that was said but to her shock, the child was dead again.

About another year passed and she conceived, now it was a series of prayers and fasting for the couple since they had already encountered two losses. When the delivery time was due, she had to sum up courage but it was even a tougher battle. Soon the baby was out alive but that was not the end of the story, the child was discovered to have breathing problems and shortness of blood. The child continued to receive care until it was announced to her that the child died again after the eight day. At this time, it was devastating for her and her husband. They had to change their numbers, addresses and many of their data because of shame and bad memories they could not stick with. These 3 losses shook their faith in God because they were praying previously. They got Pastors to join them and they cried unto God in five days vigil every week. They felt exhausted spiritually, mentally and financially so much that they had no place to retreat to other than God. Funmi made her mind not to get pregnant anymore until someone advised her to try for the last time.

She took in and her friend directed her to RCCG Maternity Centre, Ebute-Meta instead of the other hospitals she used to go to. She came to the Holy Ghost Congress and reported the case to God under the ministration of Pastor Adeboye. Nine months came and passed and her delivery was due, this time she knew God would have to pull through for her. It was on the day after Christmas in 2007, her waters broke and she went to RCCG Maternity Centre, miraculously the baby was out after about 5 minutes without any complications whatsoever. The child till now is well, perfect and strong.

MOTHER AND CHILD HEALED OF CANCER

In February 2008, a certain woman came with her child to testify of how God had healed her and her child of cancer. She had been told that she had no womb but to the glory of God, the power of God touched her and she was delivered of a set of twins, a boy and a girl, in the United States of America. The devil got upset and decided to strike the male twin after few months. He developed what they assumed was a boil at the back of his head. It was not taken with so much seriousness but was treated as a boil until they realised that the small boil began to increase in size until it became the size of a lawn tennis ball, it kept expanding till it looked like it was taking over his skull.

When the condition became unbearable, they decided to take the child to Great Ormond Hospital, United Kingdom, a Specialist Hospital for children. Solomon, the little boy was there for two weeks as several tests were carried out on him day after day. He was transferred from one machine to the other with many needles passing through his skin. It was a great torture for his mum seeing her son in that condition. The pain increased when the news was broken to her that Solomon, her son had a form of Cancer called Langaham

Celltosis and that they will have to drill through his skull to remove the portion of the brain with the Cancerous Cell. Having heard such scary news, she called her husband who told her to bring the child to Nigeria to see Pastor and Pastor Mrs Adeboye before proceeding for the surgery. She returned to Nigeria where she was directed to Pastor Adeboye by Pastor Mrs Adeboye. She took her son and met the man of God; he prayed a simple prayer on the child in few lines and laid hands on him. After that, Pastor Mrs Adeboye also advised her to put a white handkerchief in warm water, lay it on the child's affected head and then repeat the same prayer Pastor Adeboye made 'Father this child is meant to be a child of joy, not a child of sorrow, please take this sickness away from him and let him continue to be a child of joy.' She did as she was told for two months and the cancerous cell in the shape of a ball disappeared.

" One reason why Jesus Christ is the only saviour is that of all prophets and founders of the world's religions, He alone died and resurrected. While the others are dead, He lives. "
- Enoch Adeboye -

She took the twin boy back to Great Ormond Hospital to get a discharge certificate, when they ran their tests on Solomon, they could not believe it. Every trace had disappeared. They concluded that she had switched babies because they were a twin but she explained to them that the other twin was a girl and not a boy so she couldn't have switched the twins. They were amazed and contacted the Hospital in the United States where she was delivered of the kids and they were told that the gender was a boy and girl. Solomon's healing dumbfounded the doctors.

Few months later, while celebrating the wonders God did in her life over Solomon, she was told that she also had cancer of the breast and that she had only two weeks to treat it. She started to receive treatments and chemotherapy. As she received chemotherapy, the six cancer cells increased instead of reducing. The Oncologist was dazed and told her it was beyond them and that they had reached the limit on the chemotherapy she could receive again. Not knowing what to do, she heard that Pastor Adeboye was in the United Kingdom at the time, she found a way to him and he prayed for her rebuking the cancerous cells to their roots. To the glory of God, two days after, she went to the same Oncologist; they ran several tests on her only to discover there were no more cancerous cells in her breasts. She was given a date to come back after six months because the cancer had a 98percent chance of coming back. She has gone for multiple tests after the given date and she is totally free. God had healed her son, and she is also a living testimony.

CHILD GETS HEALED THROUGH NEWSPAPER

A particular brother named Mobolaji Adekunle testified of how God healed his son. After the boy was born, it was discovered that he had only one testicle instead of two. The doctors said the only way was to operate on the child before a new testicle could develop. Besides, the child was in so much pain but they trusted God for a miracle.

It was the end of the year, Watch Night service of year 2007 at the Redemption Camp; Pastor Adeboye began to minister healing and deliverances to those that needed it. It was a glorious time. He asked people to get handkerchiefs as he prayed on them and prophesied that sick would be healed when they were touched with the handkerchiefs. Mobolaji did not have a handkerchief; all he had was a newspaper he had been reading. He stretched his faith and used the newspaper as his handkerchief. Pastor Adeboye prayed on it and he went home.

On getting home, he wanted to practice the word of God's servant, so he stretched the newspaper on the floor and laid the child on it and prayed for his miracle. He continued this exercise and on the

20th day exactly, the boy got a new testicle without any surgery or medical help.

SAVED IN THE PRISON

In 2001, Mr Kingsley was sent on an errand with another gentleman. When they were to get to the other side, Mr Kingsley advised that they should walk through the Pedestrian Overhead Bridge although it seemed longer. The other guy refused and was bent on crossing the highway while Kingsley used the footbridge to the other side. Unfortunately, when Kingsley got to the other side of the road, he realised the other guy had been knocked down by a hit and run vehicle and died instantly. He was shocked and was the only eye witness that knew where the guy was from. After the guy was rushed for help, Kingsley was forced to take the bad news to the family of the guy. On getting there, he was arrested. He was arraigned before the court and after flimsy reasons were given, he was charged for murder and sentenced to Maximum Kirikiri Prison. He was kept there for several years unjustly.

In February 2002, he dreamt and saw Pastor Adeboye telling him to give his life to Christ. After he sought counsel, he started attending RCCG Prison Fellowship. About a year later, he was asked to Pastor the Prison Fellowship in his particular cell, the cell comprised of people between 50 and 90 in number. He continued for years until he had another revelation that Pastor Adeboye told him, 'your freedom has come.' He was given a key to open the door. In March 10 2008, he was called to court and the judge miraculously discharged and acquainted him. This was how he got his freedom back from unlawful imprisonment.

FROM GENOTYPE SS TO AA

God is often moved by our faith and not by sentiments. This Moslem boy called Usman was invited to a Bible club in the area he lived. After hearing of the goodness of God and the love of Jesus, faith rose up in him and he did not like the reports he was getting. Usman was born with Sickle Cell Anaemia which made his genotype SS, usually, nothing could ever change his blood so he had to live with the condition. Week by week, he noticed he was not like the other healthy children; he was always thrown in and out of the hospital. One day, he got the shocker of his life when he went with his parents to see the doctor, he overheard them saying he

> " Applying toys produce 'toy results.' Using the real keys produce 'real results.' Migrate from 'toy praying' into 'real praying.' Use your key to lock out fear and worry. "
>
> - Enoch Adeboye -

would soon die. He was barely ten years old and he knew he was not ready to die yet.

One day, when he went to the Bible club, he told his Bible teacher, a member of the Redeemed Christian Church of God, to kindly ask God to give him reasons he should die so young after so much pains. The Bible teacher encouraged him not to worry but invited him to the One week Holy Ghost Convention Pastor Adeboye held in 2007. He told his parents and was permitted to go with the teacher to the meeting. On the first day, the teacher got scared when he realised he could not find Usman, they looked for him for over two hours until when he later returned. He said he went to the Altar to lie and pray begging God to let him live long. They kept attending the programmes and listening to the word of God day after day until the fourth day when Usman disappeared again. This time he had gone to find the office of Pastor Adeboye, walked in and asked to be given a pen and paper, and he wrote in few words that Pastor Adeboye should pray for him so that he will not die young. He dropped the prayer request and left. On the fifth day being a Friday, Usman decided to join the General Fast Pastor Adeboye had proclaimed. After the programme, he felt his prayers had been answered and he told his Bible teacher that God had healed him.

When they got home, he urged his Moslem parents to please take him back to the hospital to do another test. After much persuasion, they agreed reluctantly. They were stunned when the results came out to read that Usman was no longer Sickle Cell Anaemic but his genotype had become AA. Immediately, his parents gave their lives to Christ and have joined the saints in worship. Praise God.

0.5 MILLION DOLLARS DEBT
CANCELLED IN 24HOURS

This particular brother had been involved in a business which cost about half a million dollars. The funds were loaned from his friend who trusted him dearly. Unfortunately, the business was fruitless and he eventually lost everything leaving him bankrupt. When there was no hope for the business, he told his friend that loaned him but the friend was so furious with him. He tried all he could to try to raise a little fund but it was all to no avail and everything went from bad to worse. Soon the shock got to him and his health began to fail him.

He came to the Communion Service on a Thursday, in the Redemption Camp under the ministration of Pastor Adeboye. Pastor Adeboye on the particular day told everyone to pray to God to remove sorrow and poverty from them. The brother prayed fervently. The next day, when he chose to fast and pray, he suddenly heard his phone ring. It was his old friend that loaned him the money for the business; fear gripped his heart as he picked the call. However, instead of threats, his friend told him that the debt of half a

" The rich that will make it to Heaven are those who have placed comfort in its rightful place - under their control. "
- Enoch Adeboye -

Pastor Enoch Adeboye and the love of his life, beams with smiles in gorgeous African attire.

Pastor Adeboye looks carefully at a passage in the Bible during the convention 2008.

God's messenger of joy, Pastor Enoch Adeboye spreading the love and joy of the Lord.

Pastor and Pastor Mrs Adeboye takes a group picture with the board of the Apostles Fellowship International during the 2009 Apostles conference hosted by Pastor Adeboye in Lagos, Nigeria.

Pastor Enoch Adeboye exchanging pleasantries with some of the delegates of the 2009 Apostles conference hosted by Pastor Adeboye in Lagos, Nigeria.

Taking a challenging gaze, Pastor Adeboye is doing what he was born to do as he holds the microphone firmly.

A distant view of the massive altar estimated to the size of a football pitch.

Sea of humanity in one of Pastor Adeboye's ministrations yearning for a touch from God.

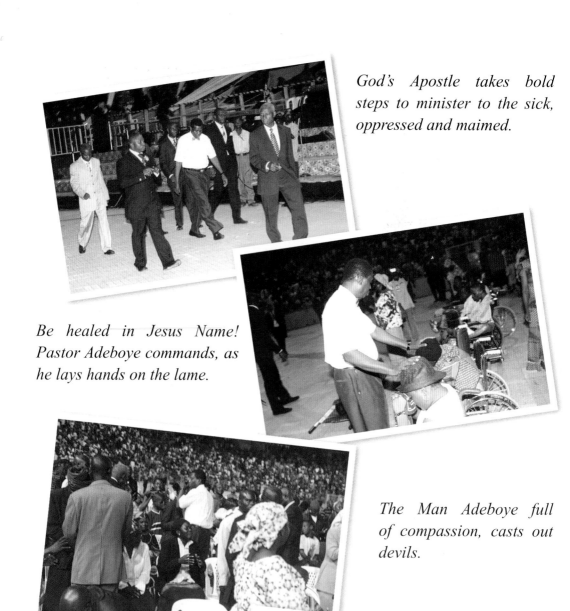

God's Apostle takes bold steps to minister to the sick, oppressed and maimed.

Be healed in Jesus Name! Pastor Adeboye commands, as he lays hands on the lame.

The Man Adeboye full of compassion, casts out devils.

The lame walk and the sick demonstrate their healing. What A God!

Wow! The son of the King of kings, Pastor Adeboye smiling confidently in Royal African Attire.

My tomorrow shall be alright, Pastor Adeboye prays as he ministers to God.

Pastor Adeboye gazes in deep thoughts of the goodness of God.

The beautiful couple, Pastor Adeboye and his wife stand by each other for life.

million dollars had been written off and that they needed to meet to do some more business. There was a great for this brother which he could not explain. He was overjoyed and has begun to move from one level of financial blessing to the other.

Chapter

14

The Man
Enoch Adeboye

When a man is called unto the high calling of God in
Christ Jesus, he is taken through the fire seven times,
pruned, purged and purified. Friend, if you wish to shine
as a vessel of gold in the great house of Master Jesus,
you must be ready to put aside the old man and all
its ways and seek always to be like Christ Jesus in
virtue, character and in chastity. Pastor Adeboye's
life is daily being renewed by Christ which is one of
his greatest success secrets.
In this chapter, you can learn from Enoch's footsteps
how he enjoys and handles his everyday life. You will
discover the wealth of wisdom he exhibits
in dealing with relationships and people in general.

Chapter

14

**The Man
Enoch
Adeboye**

Finding the right words to describe Pastor Enoch Adejare Adeboye is one of the most difficult challenges anyone would face in a writing contest. He has so many sides which makes one conclude that Pastor Adeboye's life explains what it means to be made in the image and likeness of an unpredictable and unfathomable God. In my own words, I would say Enoch Adeboye is a multi-faceted genius with a perfect blend of passion and purpose.

PLEASED TO MEET YOU SIR

You cannot but be pleased to meet this gentle servant of God. Of course, we meet people every day and while leaving we utter the above words but we know in the actual sense that what we said was far from what we meant. However, if you need to mean those words in a lifetime, then you should find a way to meet Enoch Adeboye. This 6feet 2inches tall, dark, handsome preacher walks around daily with an aura of peace and tranquillity. Although he carries a stern face that reflects a sober look in his simple short sleeve French suits yet he captures his environment with a deep baritone voice. Around the grand vibes the name "Pastor Adeboye" sends when mentioned in today's world lies this humble, simple and compassionate legend. He is a man that always leaves a lasting and unforgettable impact in the life of those that get a life time opportunity to meet him. He possesses many unknown sides which only people close to him can testify but the bottom-line is that he has a genuine love for Jesus and for souls. His reading ability is unequalled. He stays hours upon hours studying the Word of God and listening to Christian tapes. His library has books filled in excess of fifty thousand. His favourite television channel is Discovery Channel where the human mind struggles to understand God's infinite wisdom revealed in nature.

I BELIEVE IN DIVINE HEALTH

Pastor Adeboye, who is known as the holiness preacher is a man who believes in divine health. Since the Lord delivered him from series of malaria fever when he got saved, he has since been living in God's divine health.

However, behind all the spiritual activities lies a man who lives healthy. He does not believe one should abuse his body and then start demanding for healing later. He believes in living healthy and keeping your body by eating the right diet and doing physical exercise. As an unsaved undergraduate, Adeboye was a gangster and he loved boxing as a sport. He would be in the ring everyday practicing boxing and learning new skills. No one could be a successful sportsman without giving himself to physical exercise. So Adeboye was used to physical exercise because he needed to be fit. However, when he got saved he thought it was a waste of time only to discover the Bible approves of it by saying, 'bodily exercise profiteth little', (I Timothy 4:8). Since there was a little profit there, Adeboye decided to enjoy it as well. He went to the sauna to get the little profit, only to discover that, a place people rushed in and out in minutes took him over one hour to get any sweat out of his body. At that point, he knew he was in for trouble with his body because that meant to him that he had completely frozen on his inside.

From that moment on, he compulsorily put himself to physical exercise. He usually goes on prayer walks for several hours every day, walking or cycling through several kilometres, exercising his body and spirit simultaneously.

He does not eat junk meals but always makes sure his meal when not fasting are balanced and he eats a lot of fruits and vegetables.

HEALTH CHALLENGES

He enjoyed total health and body fitness until these incidents happened to him. He testified that at one of the massive Holy Ghost services where hundreds were healed, he was almost losing his hearing in one ear. When the pain was getting unbearable, he didn't mind losing his hearing partially but he just needed the pain to leave desperately. He continued trusting God for his healing while month after month thousands at the crusades testified how they had been healed when he prayed for them. It continued until someone came out to give a testimony in the regular crusade and said God had spare body parts in heaven for us. It was at that instance that Adeboye received his complete healing.

" Complete preparation packages children for progressive future outings. "
- Enoch Adeboye -

Another challenge came in his health when he suddenly was plagued by boils. About seven boils stuck to his skin in sensitive parts of his body. He could not sleep, sit or move comfortably because the pains were extremely overwhelming. To make matters worse, it was another time for the service where hundreds of thousands were waiting to be ministered to and he had to be there. He endured the pain and gradually managed to the pulpit where he ministered mightily. As he was about to step down the podium, the hand of God touched him and he was miraculously relieved of the seven boils.

I LIVE STRESS FREE

One of the most amazing misconceptions about Adeboye is that he is always keeping a stern look. Some even think he is too serious minded thinking of great visions that he cannot afford to laugh or be merry. Pastor Enoch Adeboye is a man that lives a worry free and stress free life. In contrast to the general belief, he could be very hilarious and has a fantastic sense of humour. He spices up his environment with hilarious statements and funny personal real life issues. There are no boring moments with him. He is down to earth, lively and open to a fault.

JOYOUS SENSE OF HUMOUR

Adeboye is a man full of joy and he makes it very infectious. If you ever get a chance to see him amongst his very close family members and friends, you probably might need to be carried home because the laughter and joy may be so much that you may not be able to stand. These close people know that the only thing it takes to make him release the laughing gas and joy infection in the air is to share a joke. Once the laughter from the joke is dying down, get ready because Pastor Adeboye will not wait till the next second before he starts releasing more and more jokes till everyone goes into several bursts of laughter and joy.

In his messages, he would make fun of himself to sometimes millions of people in the meetings. He said at a time, that 'he was answering the call of nature in the bush'. Although he has accomplished great feats, he is still very simple.

YOU ARE ALL GOING TO HELL IF

Adeboye making fun of his zeal without knowledge said he remembered when he just got saved; he was invited to preach to some University students. He was so excited and honoured being a lecturer. In the heat of the sermon, he told the students that anyone whose father was not born again was on his way to hell fire. He told them it did not matter if they were born again or not, they would still go to hell because God is a jealous God and he will visit the iniquities of fathers upon children even unto the third and fourth generation. The students looked amazed but Adeboye got more confident thinking he was expounding deep revelations to them.

After the sermon, one of the students raised his hand for a question and Adeboye permitted him. The student referred lecturer Adeboye to Ezekiel 18 where God said, it is the soul that sins that will die and his son will live if the son is righteous. Quoting him while remembering this incident, he said, "I did not know what was written in Ezekiel 18 because I had not read the book at all. I was only operating on the Ten Commandments. I nearly disappeared into the ground." I'm sure Adeboye wished he did not allow any public questions; at least the embarrassment might have been personal.

THE MAN WITH FRACTURED BONES

He relayed the incident when he went to the hospital to pray for someone who had been admitted in an Orthopaedic Hospital. The man had a terrible accident and had fractures in his hands, legs and ribs. On getting in, Pastor Adeboye realised the tension in the atmosphere was too tense as everyone looked too sober and sorrowful. There was no way Adeboye would pray in such an environment because there would be hardly any response.

> " If you desire anointing or you are already anointed, never compromise a life of holiness. "
> - Enoch Adeboye -

Looking for a way to cheer the visitors up, he looked at the sick man facing the ceiling, whose legs were hung up, body unmovable and all wrapped in white P.O.P (Plaster of Paris). Pastor Adeboye said humorously that since the man was constantly looking upwards, that his prayers would ascend more quickly to God than from others. Right before his eyes, people began to giggle and even the sick man who was definitely not deaf grinned because they did not expect any funny statements in that serious environment. He followed by saying the man's white garment (bandage) would make the most dressed bride jealous. Then it was an outburst of laughter everywhere even amongst the nurses. By then, when he started praying, there were resounding 'Amen' responses from everybody. The man was later discharged after he was healed.

HEAVEN HERE I COME

He reiterated on an incident when the aircraft he was on could not release its' landing gears. He said, he quickly scanned through his life to be sure his making heaven was at least sure. That seemed okay because he remembered that God wanted to tell him something before he got down from the plane so definitely, him and God were still in good terms of relationship. Suddenly while he was speaking to God, the landing gears popped out and they had a safe landing. The interesting part was not the gears that popped out but the openness of such great man of faith to be humble enough to let us know we are all human.

YOU ARE MERE DUST

One of the most known facts about Pastor Adeboye is that he is humility personified. The true test of humility is not proven when a man brags about his own humility or when a man is in a less advantaged position. It can be tested when people around you, friends, family and enemy cannot deny that you are level headed. Humility is not a facial outlook, it is in the heart. When one of the biological sons of Adeboye was interviewed and was asked what he thought was the strongest point of his father's life, his answer was not farfetched, "my dad is a very humble man and keeps teaching us to be humble." His personal secretary also said, he had never met someone more humble than Adeboye considering the heights God has taken him to. His staffs, friends, associates and the everyday Christian have all come to see the reflection of the humble spirit in Christ evident in his life as well.

Reflecting on his early life, he had problems with pride because he had risen from an unidentifiable village to become a University Graduate, obtain a Masters Degree, pursuing a Doctorate Degree, lecturing and having glaring prospect of becoming the youngest Vice Chancellor in Africa. His shoulders were high, no one had reached that point in his entire native town talk less of his family. However, when the Lord saved him, he became a pupil under an unschooled illiterate which humbled him a lot. He was also forewarned by God while standing on a beach that if he thought himself to have reached any point in life by his wisdom and became filled with pride, he would be wiped out of the surface of the earth. This combined experience made him know he had no choice other than totally yield to the person of the Holy Spirit to be his helper and to break and remould him. He constantly subjects his flesh to the power of the Holy Spirit so that Christ would he seen more and more in him.

" What you have which you consider useless may be the solution you need. "
- Enoch Adeboye -

He always said that the Lord taught him never to seek greatness or fame. He said, he only sought God with all is heart and God rewarded him with greatness. He intentionally strips himself of honour to kill his flesh daily, he would prefer to be called a child of God that his titles of Reverend Doctor or Pastor.

MAN OF COMPASSION AND GENEROSITY

Pastor Adeboye being a man who puts his absolute trust in God is a great man of faith. He believes whatever God says would come to pass under any circumstance. He trusted God to the point that when he prayed and you did not get your answer, then the problem was from man and not God. His faith was stone hard, nothing moved it, he could believe for anything. This explains the uncountable miracles which God has used him to perform because he could dare to trust God. The secret behind his faith is his genuine love and compassion for people. He loves to see smiles on the faces of people that came with pain.

This compassion for people increased when God tried him with the situation of his handicapped daughter for 22 years. The case of the ill child was part of the reason he joined the Redeemed Church of God, hoping God will heal his daughter but year in, year out, they kept believing God and serving God, no more for what they were to get but now because they loved Jesus. He would have to rise to the height of ministering healing to hundreds of thousands of people and would have to daily go back home to meet his handicapped daughter still sick. God used the situation to train him and make him feel the pains people had to carry. So when he saw those pains relieved, he could imagine the unspeakable joy that was in their hearts. God trained him for 22 years with the health condition of his third child, until he finally took her home to be with the Lord. Ever since then, seeing the agonies and pains of people and hearing their hurts could move Adeboye to tears.

Coupled with this compassion lies a great love in him. He shares contagious love with his staff, members and family at the same time and no one lacks. He shared the story of a woman who came for his meeting. She had been married for several years without a child. However, in Africa, it was a thing of shame for particularly the woman in a home to be barren. It is not usually taken lightly because it is believed that the generation of the man would be cut off if there was no child to continue the lineage. This woman's case had become so bad that the family members of her husband had become combative and confrontational with him. They had threatened to come to their home and move her things out by themselves if she did not get pregnant.

> " It is not the length or gymnastics of prayer that compels God to action; it is your ability to base your request on His word. "
> - Enoch Adeboye -

When she came to the meeting, she was broken, agonised, desperate and in tears. Adeboye recollects that when he set his eyes on her and heard her situation, he was also moved to tears. He prayed for her and asked God to give her a miracle. Not long after, God opened her womb and blessed her with a baby boy.

Besides, Pastor Adeboye is a man known with generosity. There is nothing too big for him to give out. As he gives to God, he does not relent in helping the helpless, giving to the poor, taking care of widows and God has been faithful in blessing him in return. He would take up sponsoring people who could not afford financing their education; he awards scholarships to others in Primary, Secondary and Tertiary schools. Besides, he does not hesitate to help the people that come in contact with him; he gets personally involved in the weddings, funerals of people's loved ones.

MAN OF PRAYER, PRAISE AND FASTING

Enoch Adeboye is a man of prayer and fasting. His children say they can count on their fingers, days when he is not fasting. Before many major crusades which attracts millions of souls, Adeboye sometimes denies himself of food for lengthy days. His kids sometimes get scared with the way he fasts for long days. And because of his tall frame, he can hardly stand and they sometimes feared he might break down. For many years, he formed the habit of going on his prayer walk with a long stick or staff which he uses to support himself instead of falling over for weakness in his body. He sometimes fast for forty days and nights presenting the petitions of people to God in prayer. According to the word of God, he believes that certain afflictions cannot leave except through fasting and prayer.

Prayer vigil for him is a daily activity. He goes on long prayer walks around the Redemption city for sometimes 4-5 hours talking to God. Usually, more than three quarters of his prayers are usually filled with thanksgiving and appreciation to God. He would thank God from the tiniest miracle to the everyday benefits people take for granted. His prayers usually are filled with rejoicing to God. Sometimes, he feels tired in his body but he would not allow the flesh to control him. There were other times that he would be so determined to pray all night but would fall asleep intermittently. When the sleep becomes uncontrollable, he doesn't retire to bed, instead, he gathers hard stones on the floor and kneel on it. By doing this, the stones are painful and uncomfortable so this would definitely keep him awake to pray all night. At other times, when he does not kneel on stones, he would start climbing stairs up and down in prayer. Praying in the spirit is another aspect he loves. He would pray in tongues for hours and hours. He pays so much sacrifices and he is glad at doing it.

ONCE UPON A TIME

Adeboye is a story teller; he tells personal stories, fictions and others to pass his message across when preaching to his disciples. Apart from being a story teller, he is also a poet and he is extremely good in literature. He compiled a chant of praise called "Ewi" (Praise Chant) which was a literary work depicting the magnanimity of the Almighty. Like Jesus, Adeboye speaks in parables, sometimes words of wisdom and everyone would understand.

A major strength of Enoch Adeboye is that he is always looking ahead. From the young age of eight, he knew what he wanted

> " Your request determines the size of your blessing: Ask big, receive big. Ask small, receive small. "
>
> - Enoch Adeboye -

and he was ready to pursue it. He went on hunger strike for days to convince his parents about how desperate he wanted to go to school. He discovered very early that the only way he could climb out of the poverty pit he was born into would be through education. In the process, there were challenges but he pressed forward. This same attitude is evident in his everyday life, he never sits in pity over a failure, and he always looks forward. His focus cannot be shifted and his determination goes pass the ordinary. For him, impossible does not exist.

One day when Adeboye was trying to tell his followers how to move with focus, and look ahead, he told this story;

There were two kings of two different kingdoms. There was a young one and an older king. The younger king had groups of advisers who were always hailing and praising him. At every opportunity they told him how great he was and he was very pleased. One day, his advisers and counsellors told him that he had to overcome a greater kingdom under the older king so that he could expand his domain.

He soon agreed and went to war against the bigger kingdom. The older king warned him to stay off but his advisers were adamant and he listened to them. The older king being wiser simply instructed his army to capture the younger king. Before the young king could launch attack, he was captured and taken to the other kingdom before the king. He began to beg the older in fear of being killed, claiming it was not his fault but his advisers that prompted him to do such a thing.

The king promised to release him only if he passed a test. Here was the test:

He had to transfer a brim full cup of water from one end of a stadium to the other without spilling a drop. On one side of the stadium would be people cheering and hailing him, while on the other side would be people cursing, discouraging and insulting him. Behind him was a beheader who would chop off his head the moment a drop of the water spilled on the floor. That seemed a difficult task because the water in the cup was full to the brim but he had no option. The test began, the young king scared to the bones gradually carried the water till he reached the other end. The older king on the other end asked him if it was the people praising him or the people cursing him that motivated him to transfer the cup safely. He was so honest to tell the king that he did not even know they were there because his full concentration was on his destination. Then the king told him never to listen to the praises or curses of people, he must keep his eyes always on the mark and prize. That is the path to greatness.

CLEANLINESS INSIDE OUT

Pastor Adeboye is impeccable when it comes to cleanliness. He loves a clean environment and this does not allow him to spare his driver with the car. On getting into the car or office, he would deep his hand into hidden portion where you least expect to check if it is clean. If it is dusty, then it means you need to get to work. He does not want to sight the slightest speck of dust on his dashboard or table.

Besides outward cleanliness, he is known for maintaining a holy life and abstaining consciously from any sight of sin. He has raised a standard of holiness which he holds with his life. He believes that we can attain holiness by the grace of God. He jealously guards his heart against the pollution from this world that comes from all angles. For him, Heaven is the ultimate. He repeatedly emphasizes that he would not want to live a day longer than necessary if he would do a thing that will make him miss Heaven, then God should take him home the day before.

> " If you tremble at God's word, enemies, situations and circumstances will tremble at your word. "
>
> - Enoch Adeboye -

He believes that holiness is not much of doing but rather of being. It takes deep sacrifice and conscious denials. However, it is practicable and possible to be holy. Adeboye not only lives holy, he also teaches others to pursue holiness with all their hearts and minds. It takes a willingness to obey and conquer desires of the flesh. He teaches that one must be dead to flesh and its entire works and till now, he has been a perfect example for many years. Don't be fooled, holiness has great lasting gain.

His strong addiction to holy living has made him so heaven conscious. One thing Pastor Adeboye claims not to put at risk would be his chances of making heaven. Heaven is the ultimate to him and would not compromise his spiritual standards. He would rather stay off something he is not sure would or would not hinder him from making heaven than take such things for granted and on getting to heaven realise it was a flimsy mistake. Nothing is too big in this world that can replace the joy, peace and eternal consolation in heaven. He constantly reminds his members that heaven is the height and everyone must strive to be there.

Chapter

15

Leadership Style Of Enoch Adeboye

The true test of a lasting leadership is not in how much
of command one gives but it lies in the leader giving himself
as an exemplary standard of those things which he wants
his followers to do. The world does not need a motto to say
but the world needs a model to see, that is why Apostle Paul told
the early Church to imitate him as he imitates Christ.
Leadership by example is Christ's method of effective leadership.
As a leader of the world's fastest growing denomination,
Pastor Adeboye has set himself as a good example to follow
as he follows Christ. He does not require from the people
of God those standards which he himself has not
through the help of the Holy Spirit fulfilled.

Chapter

15

Leadership Style Of Enoch Adeboye

At the heart of every grand achievement lies the soul of a leader. All the major actors of history have learned to master the art of leadership. Leadership is that inspiration which propels others to perform beyond their perceived limits. Great empires rise and fall with leadership. Whether it be political such as Nelson Mandela leading the black race in South Africa to liberation from the oppressive apartheid government or religious such as Martin Luther the reformer contending for the faith, the truth is, there can be no real achievement of outstanding exploits in isolation of visionary leadership. In order to decipher and fully comprehend the secrets behind such great achievements, it is imperative for us to first grasp the dynamics of its leadership. Despite the fact that there are universal principles of leadership such as vision, integrity, focus and the likes which all successful leaders adhere to, however careful study have proven that each leader is unique in their approach to and application of these principles. In the light of the above, for us to be more inspired by the great things which the Lord is doing around the world through his servant, it is important for us to explore what I call the Leadership Style of Enoch Adeboye.

The leadership responsibility of Pastor Adeboye is versatile. In his capacity as the General Overseer of the Redeemed Christian Church of God, he has over two hundred thousand Pastors under him. He is the President of Christ the Redeemer's Ministries, an international outreach ministry. He is the Chancellor of Redeemer's University of Nations. He is also at the helms of affairs of many other organisations within and outside the scope of the Church both nationally and internationally.

Right from his days in the academic world, Adeboye had been in leadership at various capacities. He understood the secular approach to leadership, which was based on position and rights. As a senior lecturer, he had control over the staff members and the students who were under him. Though he was young, everyone looked up to him and respected him because he had Ph.D in Applied Mathematics.

In 1973, when he gave his life to Christ, Adeboye was introduced to another kind of leadership. Just like Moses who was learned in all the wisdom of Egyptians and was mighty in words and in deeds was transported by divine providence from being the prince of Egypt to become a shepherd and to learn the principles of spiritual leadership under Jethro the priest of Midian, God also sent Enoch Adeboye to the University of the Spirit where he was tutored under the leadership style of Jesus. His mentor was Pa Akindayomi, a complete illiterate who did not have any formal education and could not even speak English language. Under the stern spiritual leadership of Pa Akindayomi, the young University don had to completely empty himself of his previous leadership ideologies and receive lessons from his spiritual mentor. The nature of the assignment which God had for him was spiritual, so Adeboye had to learn the intricacies of spiritual leadership from a man who though did not have formal education was versatile in the ways of God. It was during those years of rigorous training that Pastor Adeboye formed a new style of leadership which is helping him today to accomplish the great work of the Kingdom around the world.

THE TEN LEADERSHIP STYLE OF ENOCH ADEBOYE ONE: HOLINESS.

Leadership experts call it integrity, others call it credibility but Pastor Adeboye prefers to call it holiness and it's first on the list of his leadership strategies. For him holiness is also simple obedience. Obedience is doing what one's master instructs without question or grudge. Hence, no matter what sphere of business you find yourself, you must be willing to be submissive and obedient to

> " Eagles eat live chickens, vultures eat dead animals. Believers are spiritual eagles, unbelievers are like vultures. What do you eat? "
>
> - Enoch Adeboye -

the authority placed over you. Obedience and integrity has its own great reward.

There was a time when they had planned for the congress to be held in Benin, a southern part of Nigeria but God told him to change it to Ede, a smaller city in the western part of Nigeria. He obeyed and the meeting was held in Ede. From the miracles in the congress, God touched the heart of the king of the land, a Moslem, and he blessed the Church with a 500 hectares piece of land all for no cost.

Early on in his Christian walk, Adeboye learnt from his spiritual father that we cannot achieve any spiritual exploit without holiness. Pa Akindayomi, Adeboye's mentor was a man of adamant holiness and frowned at any trace of sin and unrighteousness and had imparted the same values in Adeboye. For them, the only way to true greatness is holiness. He believes we can attain perfection by the grace of God. One's ability to be holy could be difficult but God can use man's readiness. Although, he warns that holiness should be a lifestyle and a means to an end not an end in itself. Making holiness an end could lead to self righteousness which is not healthy. For several years, people have built great confidence in Pastor Adeboye. Not just the leaders of RCCG or members but the average Christian and the ordinary man on the street of Nigeria have all come to submit to him as a holiness figure. Over time, he has maintained a high level of credibility by intentionally detaching and separating himself from the demands and pleasures of this present age. He has always set the example.

TWO: HUMILITY

Pastor Adeboye is one person who believes in the principle of abasing oneself. He is of the belief that he has achieved nothing by reason of his wit, sharpness or expertise but it is all by the grace of God. True humility for him, should be expressed and not just be a thing of the secret heart. He would prefer to humble himself in a place with quietness until the day he is discovered. This virtue which he consciously worked on has helped him a great deal. While referring to himself when preaching to over 7 million people, he calls himself a child of God. Rather than taking on the several titles that he deserves, he chooses to remain simple. This simplicity finds its way into the heart of his followers making them comfortable to follow him. For instance, when he was chosen to take over the ministry from his predecessor, Pa Akindayomi who had died, although he was ordained as a Reverend Doctor and the portfolio of the new office was General Superintendent, however, when he realised the title and position would make his new followers uncomfortable, he changed it. He picked to be called Pastor and General Overseer instead.

His personality, character and way of life all point towards stripping oneself of honour, giving it to God and you will find it coming back to you. Pastor Adeboye has a great leadership quality that makes him able to clarify his values and express himself. His humility style complements his strong beliefs of holiness, which make him able to lead anyone, even lions if they were placed under him.

THREE: VISION

Pastor Adeboye's foresight cannot be ignored. It forms the basis of many of the great feats God has used him for. He could take a glimpse ahead and envision the future. His dynamic attitude makes it possible for him to adapt to the developments of this age and use it as a tool for the gospel. From every circumstance of life, he saw a future in it. When he was a young boy, he knew if he had not chosen education, he would not have risen above his father's occupation of farming. The vision he saw was different and he was willing to pursue it. For instance, he was going one day as a youngster, suddenly he saw a car pass by. One person, the chauffeur was driving and the other person sat comfortably and was being driven. When he looked at the two scenarios, he realised that one was being served. So, at such a young age, he decided that he would be that person sitting comfortably and being driven. He had focus, goals and targets which he worked towards. Everything he does at a particular season is geared towards the main whole which is his vision. He is unmoved by the things around him, he follows his heart and walks alone.

His focus on the things he chooses to do is unflinching. He does not get carried away by the praises of his followers neither does he respond to the voice of his critics. He is always on the move to destiny.

> " If you endure rather than enjoy being in the house of God, it is an indicator of dying Pentecostal fire. "
> - Enoch Adeboye -

> " Anointing attracts open doors just as magnet attracts metals. "
> - Enoch Adeboye -

Taking a flashback to the very moment he took over the mantle of leadership of the Church, he moved from one vision to another vision without considering the oppositions he might face. He never focuses on the past, he always looks ahead. His forward looking ability in times of rapid change differentiates him from other leaders.

FOUR: DETERMINATION

Pastor Adeboye is a man of strong determination. When he decides to do something that he is convinced about, nothing can stop him. He leads by example, his psychological hardness is unequalled, he never backs out of a vision regardless of how impossible things appear to be. He has an in-built and God-given die-hard attitude. The determination he exhibits is evident when he chose to go to school, he chose not to eat for three days until the vision became a reality. When he became a leader of the Church, he did not mind spending his last dime to see that any set vision manifested. He could work so hard and never took no for an answer. One interesting aspect of his determination is that he adds a level of urgency to it.

In his words, he shares his belief,

"When God gives you an urgent urge to do something it could mean that if you do not do it at that particular time, it would never be done. I remember very well, when we were going to build our international office, God made it clear to me that the office must be built that month and I wondered how I will do it. I felt that urgency in my spirit so I called the engineer working with me and told him that I wanted to build an office with about thirty rooms and it was to be done in three weeks. I said I wanted it to be a three-week wonder. He looked at me as if something must be wrong with me. I drew what I wanted on paper. The engineer asked for the surveyor's plan and I said the surveyor would meet us by the time we finish. Now when I look back, if the office had not been built that month, probably I would not have been able to build it because just as I finished the building, there came many urgent needs for money. However, in the meantime, the office is there."

FIVE: SEIZE OPPORTUNITIES

If there is another name for Pastor Adeboye, it would be a man who recognises opportunities and seizes the moment. From a little boy, when he realised a school was opening in their local village, he chose to seize the moment. Also while in University, he heard of the benefits that were being given to people in sports so he jumped on the information and made sure he did everything possible to outshine other people who wanted to be in the group. He constantly puts his ear to the ground, seeking information on the available opportunities. He is highly innovative and he looks out for fresh ideas for change and improvement. When it was time for the RCCG to spread, he created Model parishes to accommodate the high class strata of the society while still keeping the lower and middle class people. He was not ready to let go of any one, he adds to his spread and takes every opportunity important. He also does not jump into every door that opens, he carefully inspects and selects those that are opened by God. He shares one incident that happened to him as a young man decades ago,

> " Holiness is a fortified mansion that provides safety for all its residents. "
> - Enoch Adeboye -

"Many years ago, I was going to Canada, I was travelling on Nigeria Airways, which took off a bit late so by the time we got to London, the British Airways that was to take me to Canada had left. So they arranged for me to go and stay in a hotel. When I got there, they gave

> " If you can turn an idea from vision into reality, God will open doors to more and greater ideas. "
> - Enoch Adeboye -

me some tickets for dinner. There were two restaurants, one on the right and one on the left. I did not know which one to go to. I just said, 'When I get to Heaven, I will turn right' so I went to the restaurant on the right. I did not know that the restaurant was meant for those with First Class ticket and I had Economy ticket so I went down there and enjoyed myself. I said to myself, 'Oh God, how I wish somebody will come and take my picture now and go and show it to them in Ifewara and show them the son of Adeboye being served like a king.'"

SIX: EXEMPLARY LIVING

One great strength of Pastor Adeboye's leadership is that he leads by example and he is open. He has a way of making his followers comfortable. He does not appear hyper-spiritual and flawless rather he shares his mistakes, fears and vulnerability. This style of leadership makes his followers know that he a man of like passion. So if he could overcome some challenges, it is possible for everyone to overcome the challenges too.

In 2001 he shared with the millions of people that were in his crusade,

"Because I take God's word seriously, it has helped me to deal with certain habits in my life that were not good. An example is pride. Thank God, I read in James 4:10 that if I humble myself under the mighty hands of God, He will lift me up. I Peter 5:5-6 says, God resists the proud but gives grace to the humble. He said we should be clothed in humility. We should not just be humble but wear humility as a garment. Another thing that God settled in my life as a result of my deep respect for the word of God that is forever settled is, Anger. Proverbs 16:32 says he that is slow to anger is better than the mighty. Ecclesiastes 7:9 says anger rests in the bosom of fools. ... Therefore, I refuse to be a fool."

Also, till date, he goes on "Let's go a fishing", an outreach to integral parts of the country evangelising Jesus. He would go with his leaders in a giant bus to villages and hidden places where people do not know the saving knowledge of the cross. At times, they would stay there for days as missionaries. He would leave the comfort of his home at these times and would not hesitate to sleep in the sub standard accommodation provided in the mission.

SEVEN: TEAM PLAYER

Testimonies fly around his leaders about his fantastic ability to team play. In meetings, he has a way of blending softness and firmness. One of his first most challenging leadership opportunities was when the RCCG was handed to him. Such a task could make someone give in to fear and intimidation; he was to lead a group of elderly people who were old enough to be his parents, who were in the organisation before him, who were more experienced in the field. However, Enoch Adeboye was endowed with supernatural wisdom. He introduced trainings for them, carried them along, organised meetings and sought to improve them. Although some had to leave but those that stayed under his leadership were glad they did when they saw the results of his leadership.

He constantly makes his followers develop a shared sense of destiny. He made them part of the vision so much that if the vision fails, it would be them failing. He stays in the forefront of the vision as he confidently spells out the plan. Every member and leader is given a high sense of belonging. One irreplaceable ingredient in his team playing is 'Trust'. He does not carry the entire burden on himself but he conveniently entrusts people in position and gives them an opportunity to prove themselves. Pastor Adeboye enlists others in a common vision by appealing to shared aspirations. Since collaboration improves performance, he creates a climate of trust, facilitate positive interdependence, support face-to-face interactions, create a spirit of community and he empowers people.

" When you become born again, you start a relationship with God. That makes Him your Father. As you daily water that relationship, He becomes your Daddy. "
- Enoch Adeboye -

EIGHT: EXCELLENCE

Pastor Adeboye undoubtedly possesses the spirit of excellence. He focuses on clear standards and encourages his followers to live up to the standard.

For him, he does not think anything is impossible as long as you can conceive it. He is highly optimismistic and expects the best of the situation he finds himself. His excellent spirit makes him pay attention to his followers, he listens to their advices but he makes the decisions. He is highly intelligent and brainy in all fields, however when he does not have expertise in a particular field he is delving into, he seeks people that are experts and gets their advice and empowers them. He is not intimidated by the success of his followers instead he prays that they would be greater than him. He celebrates success and seeks to build up the people that are under him.

NINE: DISCIPLINE

Pastor Adeboye is a man who encourages hardwork but he is irritated when he meets people that are slack going nowhere. With over 200,000 Pastors under him, there are some bad eggs. Many people try to take his simplicity for granted but he does not hesitate to show his lion side. Although he corrects his followers with love yet he disciplines anyone who tends to continuously stray. He does not condemn people but brings them to God through the correction necessary.

TEN: BIG THINKER

One of the unbeatable aspects of Pastor Adeboye is that he dares to dream big. He is never satisfied with mediocrity. He is always looking ahead, going forward and thinking big. Here, from his own words below, you can see a typical example,

"There was a time when I thought a crowd of a thousand people was a large crowd. Then I travelled to America to attend Kenneth Hagin Camp Meeting and I saw 17,000 people in Church. On the plane on my way back home, I began to pray, 'God, one day I too must stand before 17,000 people'. Some years later I travelled to Korea and I saw the Church of Yonggi Cho with 450,000 people. I said, 'God, I do not want 17,000 anymore. I too want more than 450,000. If you can see it you can have it. Now I have seen something great. I have seen a time that when we want to have Holy Ghost Festival the government will declare public holiday. They will not do it voluntarily but they will have to do it compulsorily because there will be nobody left in the offices.'

After the Church grew from over 17,000 to over 450,000, you would think it is a good time for Adeboye to stay settled and satisfied until when he expanded his vision again. He said,

"Since I attended Yonggi Cho's Church in Korea, I began to expand my vision and I began to tell my Pastors that in every town, within five minutes walking distance, there must be a parish of The Redeemed Christian Church of God. They thought it was impossible but I have already seen it. However, I have already expanded my vision beyond that one. The day I heard that Coca-Cola said that very soon in every home there would be somebody who drinks Coca-Cola in the whole world, I changed my vision and I've said, in every home in the whole world, there must be a member of The Redeemed Christian Church of God. I have seen it. God said if I can see it I can have it"

Pastor Adeboye, the fantastic Team leader gives instructions to some of his leaders and graduating ministers.

Humble Enoch Adeboye, kneels and bows in worship and total surrender to God.

Daddy and Mummy G. O in close compliments with foreign Apostles in a meeting hosted by Pastor Adeboye.

Pastor Adeboye congratulating some graduating students after Bible School Training.

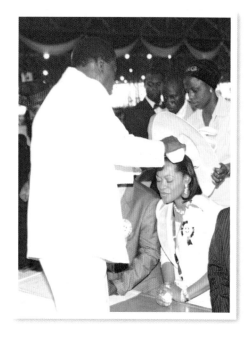

Go ye into the world! Pastor Adeboye commissions and ordains some leaders.

A man of deep humility and addicted to worship. Pastor Enoch Adeboye lies postrate to worship the Lord, the Maker of heaven and earth.

Daddy and Mummy G. O celebrating along with some family members and well wishers.

Some students of Redeemed University of Nations in front of one of their faculty buildings.

Cross section of a Building at the Redeemers University.

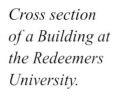

The University Guest House.

UBA Bank at the Redemption Camp

The Arts Theatre of the Redeemers University

Oceanic Bank at the Redemption Camp

Pastor Adeboye gives a look of,
'This is just the beginning',
We have not started.

Chapter

16

Oppositions
And
Criticisms

Martin Luther King Jnr. once said,
a true measure of the stature of a great man is not
if he stands in moments of comfort and convenience
but whether he still stands in those moments of
conflicts and controversy.
Just like Jesus Christ the Captain of our Salvation was persecuted,
so all that will live godly lives and fulfil their divine destiny
must suffer various persecutions.
Right from inception, the ministry and life of Enoch Adeboye has
been under severe attacks from within and outside the folds;
however, like the seed of greatness
which he is, the more they persecute him, the more the grace
and power of God in him increased unto greater works.
Enoch Adeboye feeds fat on oppositions.
If God helped him to silent the mouth of the lions and
conquer all giants, you can also thrive above all
threatening and confronting oppositions that are against
the accomplishment of your divine destiny.

Chapter

16

Oppositions And Criticisms

In May 1999, Pastor Adeboye and his lovely wife went on a trip to Jerusalem. While there, they were having a chit chat when Mummy G.O (Pastor Folu Adeboye) told her husband that she needed to get a body massage. Pastor Adeboye responded by telling her the part of his body that needed massage was his heart. This is because he had been stabbed severally and had endured much pain for the sake of the gospel of Jesus. His flesh was being crucified daily so that he would be dead to the things of the world.

One would think such a gentle, easy going, quiet and humble man that goes his own way with his God would walk through this world with no one pointing an accusing finger at him, far from it. It is not surprising because Jesus, our example, who knew no sin and lived perfectly, was also criticised and opposed.

However, in the midst of all the trials, oppositions and criticisms, one big secret of Pastor Adeboye is that he stays focused and he is never distracted by the positive or negative comments of men. It is so amazing that this man of God would consciously escape set ups of praise which people taught he deserved. His main strength lies in his dogged determination and rugged focus on the accomplishment of his God given destiny.

YOU CANNOT LEAD US

One of the interesting challenges Pastor Adeboye had as a young Pastor was that there were a lot of conservative who rose up against his new change movement. They did not want a change, they preferred to remain in their old ways of doing things and keep the traditions thereby unconsciously acting as a stumbling block to the Holy Spirit. The old traditional leaders he met in the Church did not want him to lead them. Some thought he was moving too fast for their comprehension, some thought he was too young spiritually and physically, some felt more qualified and were jealous while others thought his education was overexciting him and making him over zealous. They told him that the Church under him was like a muddy pool that would eventually dry up. These were trying times that tested his faith and everything he believed. There were series of intentional gang ups against him but God intervened and prevailed over the manipulations of Satan. Reiterating after many years,

" Everyone is born with fundamental human rights. However, only those who have conquered poverty can exercise those rights. "
- Enoch Adeboye -

"Years ago, when my father in the Lord had just died and there was little problem we had about who would succeed him, there was a meeting where all kinds of things were said about Pastor Adeboye. Half truths were dressed up as the whole truth. While this was going on, the Holy Spirit told me to keep quiet, and I kept quiet. Just at the right moment, He gave me a word of wisdom. All I said was,

'Gentlemen, remember that it is written that every idle word that any man would alter, he will give an account for it on the Day of Judgement.' This put an end to the meeting. "

ADEBOYE MUST DIE

Adeboye is not so much of a confrontational person but there was an oppressive man that was bent on terminating his life by all means. He was sent by God to deliver a message to this African leader who was a mean dictator, he murdered innocent people and sent many to their early graves. Pastor Adeboye being an influential man and a prayerful Christian leader was a threat to the evil acts of the tyrant. There was no peace for this man whenever he remembered that Pastor Adeboye was still alive especially when the message pricked his heart. He was soon manipulated by his informants that he would be free to commit all atrocities to any extent he desired if only he could kill Adeboye. The wicked man would have loved to be discreet about his mischief but he could not hide his feelings so much that the presence of Pastor Adeboye got him so irritated that everyone knew the next target.

When the news got to Pastor Adeboye, his first instinct was to pray for the man to repent from doing evil and turn to God. He continued to pray for the man everyday but the man remained adamant and sought his life. Soon, the Holy Spirit ministered to Adeboye that the man was an anti-Christ and would not relent in seeking his life. At that point, he knew it was time to take the situation to God. Before, he could reason out the next move, God took the battle to the gates of the enemy for him and the man sud-

" You are the beginning of several generations. The seeds you sow today will be harvested by generations long after you have gone. What are you sowing? "

- Enoch Adeboye -

denly slumped and died. This was how Pastor Adeboye got his total liberty and freedom.

ADEBOYE, ACCOMPANY ME TO HELL

Sometimes, when the enemy plans evil for God's chosen vessels, God has a way of turning it round for their good. In the words of Pastor Adeboye, he expresses the oppositions he received from a man who was bent on taking both of them on a roller-coaster to hell.

" A veritable way of helping yourself is by assisting the poor. "
- Enoch Adeboye -

"When I enlisted in the army of the Lord, God told me that my late father in the Lord, the Late General Superintendent was to be my immediate boss and that to whatever he said, my answer must be, 'yes sir.' I thought this was wonderful... Then I organized a programme, with his permission. The other Pastors were informed and one of the senior Pastors became angry. He thought that I wanted to show off that I was educated. So this Pastor wrote me a very nasty letter, cursing me and saying all kinds of terrible things. I ran to report to Papa and I read the letter to him. I thought he would tell me to go and bring the Pastor. Instead, he said I should go and beg the Pastor. Again, that little rebellion came up. Again the Holy Spirit cautioned me. I went and I begged him. A couple of years or so later, this same man stood up in the meeting of Pastors and said that he had made up his mind that he would be going to hell but he would take at least three people with him. I would have gone with him but for the Almighty God who put me under an officer who knew what he was doing."

ADEBOYE REFUSED TO LAY HANDS ON ME

All through his ministry, Pastor Adeboye is always accused of hoarding his anointing. With other 200,000 Pastors under his leadership, many others criticize him of not impacting into their lives the anointing on his life by laying hands on them. This has always been a contrast to the belief of Pastor Adeboye, since the Bible warned him not to lay hands suddenly on any man so that he would not be a partaker of the man's sins (I Timothy 5:22). Although many come to him requesting for impartation through laying on of his hands, some others who have their minds made up on what they want to do would also come to him to lay hands on them to approve of what he knows nothing about. Many believe all they need to make it in life and ministry is the direct prayer and laying on of hands of Pastor Adeboye regardless of whether that is the right direction God wants for them or not. Adeboye poses that he would not like to take the risk of sharing in someone's sin unknowingly. On the other hand, he believes that even if God was in approval of such a vision or person, there would be no need for him to act as a mini god to the person when he is not sent to do that. He claims that the only instance he would commission an individual is if God specifically tells him to do so.

CANCEL THE PROGRAMMES

Challenges of cancelling already announced programmes were not uncommon to Adeboye. There were many times he had set out to achieve great feats which were always above the financial resources available. His secret is that he does not keep his eyes on the impossibility of what will be required. He just sets a target according to the leading of God and believes that by the time he gets to the point of needing particular things, there will be a provision. This strategy has always worked for him. There are many that would have set out goals but would bury the vision because they get discouraged by the reports they get. This is not the case with Enoch Adeboye; he never takes impossible as an answer. He believes there must always be a way and there is always the provision waiting at the point of sacrifice. When Daddy G. O. says Go On, his leaders don't hesitate because they have seen it time and time again how they thrived even better and come out even brighter after series of these challenges. When the Holy Ghost Festival '99 was to be held at the Redemption Camp, there were discouraging challenges that stood in the way. The time frame to the meeting was so unbelievable to get the things that needed to be done. It could only have been possible by the intervention of God. The place was not prepared and the people were getting ready to come for the meeting. Pastor Adeboye had to supervise the labourers to work overnight for days constructing the place. At about two days to the hosting of the programme, there was still a need to fill up a whole twenty feet deep stream that surrounded the area the meeting was to be held. It was obvious that if people thronged in for the programme and the stream was unfilled, there would have been mass burial of people. Some people raised ideas of fencing the stream but that was too risky when people were supposed to come in their millions. Hours began to tick and everyone was under serious tension, the meeting could no longer be cancelled, it was two days more. However, in the midst of the impossible situation, Pastor Adeboye kept his calm and God gave him a solution. He ordered for all sand filling tippers from about five different states to bring in sand continuously and at the same time to fill the stream. He ordered from Lagos, Ibadan, Abeokuta, Sagamu and Ijebu Ode. As over hundreds of trucks came in with sand, they emptied it in the stream and they continued the process for over forty hours. The stream was totally safe and sand filled just about the time people were arriving for the meeting without anyone knowing the challenges they had faced.

There was a time the convention was to be held. Everything was almost in place, invitations had been sent out and people were getting ready to be in the meeting until there was a national uproar that totally disrupted the whole activities that were lined up. The country was in chaos as there was shortage of fuel, transportation and strike action. The whole system paralysed and there also seemed to be shortage of finances as regards to the things that were still undone.

When the leaders of the Church saw the position of things, they knew there was no point continuing with the plan because it seemed like the programme would still end up in a flop. There was no way for the crowd to get to the meeting no

> " In accomplishing anything in life, if the method is wrong, the result will be wrong. If the method is right, the result will be acceptable. "
> - Enoch Adeboye -

matter how desperate they want to come. Hence, they all called Pastor Adeboye and they explained the whole scenarios to him, they pointed out all the signals that pointed to the fact that the convention could not hold at the stipulated time. They confirmed to him that they were not against the meeting holding but the time they had previously set was now unrealistic. After all their analysis, Pastor Adeboye countered it with just a question. He asked them if any of them thought God had made a mistake in fixing the convention for that time. Everyone kept quiet. Since there were no more objections, they went on against all odds and the convention held. There were countless miracles in the meeting and people came with the testimonies of how they were mysteriously helped to make it to the programme. The convention of that year ended up being a huge success.

FIGHT AGAINST THE FLESH

Another opposition which Pastor Adeboye deals with brutally is the Flesh. He agreed that the flesh constantly wars against the spirit so one must make conscious effort to kill the desires of the flesh. Pastor Adeboye recalls that he met an 80 years old American widow who lost her husband few years' back, who confessed that at her age, she experienced temptations although slightly different from the younger generation, and that death is the only terminator of temptations. Hence, the point is temptations will never cease but God can bring us into a realm where we can live in constant victory over the works of the flesh. This is the place Adeboye operates from and he daily guards his heart diligently with the studying of the Word of God, listening to scriptural tapes everywhere he found himself, fasting, constant praise and prayers.

Chapter

17

Community
Development
And
Philanthropy

The gospel to the total man must meet the needs in all the
components of his being which includes spirit, soul and body.
The Lord Jesus Christ having taught the multitudes for some days
was moved by their physical needs for food and blessed bread
and fish which he multiplied to feed thousands
of men, women and children.
The Body of Christ also has the social responsibility to
cater for the poor and the needy, to feed the hungry and clothe
the naked, to provide humanitarian services to those
nations of the world that are torn apart by war, poverty and
epidemics.
Through various initiatives and programmes,
Enoch Adeboye is taking the lead to be the extension of God's
hands and feet by providing physical, social, emotional
and tangible aids to alleviate the plight of the disadvantaged.

Chapter

17

Community Development And Philanthropy

When the missionaries first brought Christianity to Africa, they held the Bible in one hand and Community Service on the other hand. They preached the Gospel to the people and they also made great positive impact on the community through education, health-care, infrastructures and other social facilities. What is referred to as missions' schools in Nigeria's modern day educational sector is the legacy left behind as proof of the social impact made by early missionaries. In the last five centuries, the story of the spread of Christianity in Africa is far more the story of African Christians spreading the Gospel in Africa than it is the story of foreign missionaries spreading the Gospel in Africa. This new trend poses a huge challenge to the leaders of the African Independent Churches to also emulate the humanitarian examples of the missionaries who brought the Gospel to the African soil and embark on com-

" A blossoming spiritual life is your immunization certificate against negative pronouncements and curses. "

- Enoch Adeboye -

" For a regular temptation a demon is sent. For an intense case an army of demons are sent. For an extraordinary case Satan himself is sent. "
- Enoch Adeboye -

munity development programs that would impact positively on the lives of their people.

To utter disdain, what is prevalent in the African Independent Churches is faith that is not backed up with works. There is ecstatic worship, aggressive prayers and preaching but it all ends there. Most of the Churches do not embark on programs and projects that would have direct impact on the physical needs of the people. Against the commands of Christ to feed the poor, clothe the naked and to care for orphans and widows, much of the African Church has isolated herself from such social responsibilities and continues to point accusing fingers at the Government. Amidst this gloomy trend, the ministry of Enoch Adeboye has ignited flames of hope.

A man who has had his own share of cruelsome poverty, who grew up under stringent conditions and having received the privilege of education at costly measures, Enoch Adeboye is particularly touched when he sees the suffering of the society, many of whom are members of his Church. He has vouched to use all opportunities at his disposal to alleviate the plight of the less privileged in the society and to create the opportunity of education for young people. Using the platform of the Redeemed Christian Church of God, Enoch Adeboye has made tremendous positive impact on the society by initiating different programs and projects that are aimed at helping the needy. The followings are some of the initiatives of the social services of the Redeemed Christian Church of God led by Pastor Enoch Adeboye.

CHRIST THE REDEEMER'S WELFARE SERVICE (CRWS)

Pastor Enoch Adeboye commissioned the CRWS on January 13, 1991. Prior to the establishment of this organization, Pastor Adeboye noticed that there were many youths in the Church who did not have employment and had to continuously solicit for support from the privileged members of the Church. Adeboye responded to the situation by creating a job employment department as an arm of the Christ the Redeemer's Friends Universal, (CRFU) an initiative previously established to reach out to the crème de la crème in the society. The initial objective of the CRWS was to help the youths to acquire various skills, link up the skilled and semi skilled youths with various employers in need of their skills and to get them employed.

The initiative became a huge success as a job placement agency. God used many committed people to expand and execute the vision. It was later carved out of the CRFU as an autonomous body within the Church and extended its scope of operations to include;

Financial support for small scale businesses

Financial support for less privileged students;

At present, a scholarship program has been launched to provide grants for students in tertiary institutions.

Financial assistance on compassionate grounds for those in need of cash to meet urgent needs and distressed situations

A home for orphans and motherless babies called Heritage Home which is situated at the Redemption City.

Missionaries Support Program

This initiative has made tremendous positive impact on the society towards the alleviation of poverty and wealth creation.

THE REDEEMED AIDS PROGRAM ACTION COMMITTEE (RAPAC)

The Redeemed Aids Program Action Committee (RAPAC) is another social services initiative of the Redeemed Christian Church of God. It is a non-profit faith based organisation established by Pastor Enoch Adeboye in May 1999 in response to the distress of those who are infected with the HIV/AIDS virus and those who are affected by it in the society. Initially, the initiative only catered for the needs of people living with HIV/AIDS but with time it expanded to include care for widows, orphans and vulnerable children and reproductive health. The objective of RAPAC is to provide detailed and up to date information, training and counselling on HIV/AIDS, sexual and reproductive health measures to members of the society, particularly women and youths and to provide support for those who are already infected with the virus, widows, orphans and vulnerable children. In order to achieve the above listed objectives, RAPAC is in partnership with other organisation with similar objectives such as United States Agency for International Development (USAID), Family Health International, Winrock International and Society for Family Health. The operations of RAPAC is into many scope which includes HIV/AIDS Prevention, HIV Counselling and Testing, Prevention from Mother to Child Transmission, Basic Care and Support through Education, Caring for Orphans and Vulnerable Children, Microfinance.

The HIV/AIDS is fast spreading in Nigeria and this is largely factored by the gross ignorance of people on the matter. Many people do not know their HIV status and those who have tested positive are too scared of being stigmatised to take advantage of the available support. RAPAC is working hard to enlighten the Pastorate, ministers, leaders, parents and young people about HIV/AIDS by organising seminars, workshops and training programs. To prevent the spread of the HIV/AIDS, RAPAC is campaigning that young people should practice absti- nence and the married couple should be faithful to their partners. To em- phasize the message, behavioural change communication materials are constantly distributed to the members of the Church and the society at large. Due to the efforts

> " Opportunities for personal blessings, often, are disguised as obligations to God. "
>
> - Enoch Adeboye -

of RAPAC, the HIV/AIDS is no more presumed as a death sentence but a disease which could be controlled. Many people who have tested positive to HIV/AIDS are living positive lives.

In 2005, RAPAC was chosen by the Global HIV/AIDS Initiative Nigeria (GHAIN) as one of the agencies to implement HIV Coun- selling and Testing Project in Lagos. This was done with the sup- port of other international organisation such as USAID. This really enhanced the work of RAPAC as free and voluntary HIV Testing and Counselling takes place everyday for everyone at the RAPAC Heart to Heart Centre in Ebute-Meta, Lagos. Children who lost their parents to HIV/AIDS are taken care of by RAPAC and sent to schools. Four of such schools have been established in four states of Nigeria, namely; Abuja, Benue, Cross-River and Oyo States. Wid- ows and single parents especially those living with HIV are trained and grants are provided for them to start businesses so that they can support their families. Through its many charity programs, RAPAC is saving lives and helping people whom otherwise might not have the hope of survival to have a chance to life.

CAMPAIGN AGAINST DRUG ABUSE MINISTRY (CADAM)

Campaign against Drug Abuse Ministry (CADAM) is a rehabilitation centre where drug addicts are evangelised, rehabilitated and reinstated back into the society. The headquarters of CADAM is at Dominion Sanctuary, the headquarters of RCCG, Lagos Province 2 which is at ACME in Ikeja. The program is co-ordinated by medical practitioners. Addicts who have passed through the program have come in through referrals by friends, family or even the public. Others came in through evangelism carried out in popular drug joints. When an addict is referred to CADAM, he or she is firstly numbered, fed well, clothed and then sent to the Liberty House in Poka near Epe, a suburb of Lagos State where they undergo a period of intensive counselling and spiritual training. After their completion of the preliminary stage, the patient would be transferred to another facility at Akute, another suburb of Lagos where they are trained in the skills of their choice to help them get integrated into the society as responsible citizens. They are allowed to continue to live at the Akute facility until they are up and standing and ready to start a new life. CADAM adopts a unique combination of the medical and psychological approach with the spiritual approach. This has produced tremendous results and helped many who were hooked on drugs to give it up and live a normal life of liberty. The organisation has become successful and numerous former drug addicts have been rehabilitated and referrals come in from all over the Country and even from outside the Country.

MATERNITY CENTRE AND HEALTHCARE CENTRE

As far back as 1952, under the leadership of the first General Superintendent Pa Akindayomi, the RCCG had opened a Maternity Centre at its small Ebute-Metta Church premises to care for the pregnant women who are members of the Church. In 1991, Pastor Adeboye took the healthcare initiative of the Church to a whole new dimension by registering the Maternity Centre and providing latest medical equipments. The RCCG is a faith based organisation and believes in the efficacy of prayers and the power of God to heal the sick. However, Pastor Adeboye understands that there are certain illnesses that require medical attention. So he made provisions for qualified medical personnel, equipments and medications to be available at the maternity centre. Many parishes of the RCCG have also opened their own maternity centres and people are admitted from everywhere. The centre has helped in the safe delivery of thousands of children all over the country. The Maternity Centre runs weekly antenatal meetings where the women are given spiritual support. There is also a big Health Centre at the Redemption City which caters for the health needs of the people.

EDUCATION - THE GENESIS

A former University don, prior to his call into the ministry, Adeboye had courted the dream of going down in history as the youngest University Vice-Chancellor in Africa. Now that he is in the service of God, he expresses his love for education by starting of different institutions of learning from the kindergarten to University. Apart from planting of Churches, another thing Adeboye enjoys doing is starting of new schools. He believes strongly that next to the salvation of the soul, education is one of the most important legacies in a man's life. Shortly after he was consecrated into office as the General Overseer of the mission, Pastor Adeboye embarked on the mission of schools. The first school which he started in 1982 was a Nursery School for little kids. He believed that if the children had the proper foundation from the beginning, it would prepare them for the journey ahead in life. His wife Pastor (Mrs.) Folu Adeboye, who already had 15 years experience in the teaching profession, took up the responsibility of running the school. The school started at the Church building in Ebute-Metta with few pupils and had only one teacher. Through the steadfast efforts of Pastor Adeboye and his wife, the primary school also took off four years later in 1986. By this time, the numbers of staff increased to five teachers and one cook. As the work progressed, more like minded people began to express their willingness to be a part of the vision to give the children sound Christian education.

THE REDEEMER'S SCHOOL MOVEMENT

Pastor Adeboye established a new initiative called Christ Redeemers School Movement and Pastor (Mrs.) Folu Adeboye became the Chairperson. The movement was commissioned to establish new schools, to create conducive atmosphere for the realization of academic excellence, to create a balanced curriculum which will gear towards the spiritual, mental, social, and physical development of pupils. The first Nursery and Primary school yielded tremendous results. The Redeemer's School Movement acquired another facility in Iwaya Lagos, to augment the little space that the school occupied at Ebute-Metta. As the Church continued to experience phenomenal growth, there was also a higher demand for Godly instruction. The Redeemer's School Movement started another school called Redeemer's International School. Later on, the School Movement began to start secondary schools. Today, there is virtually no state in Nigeria where a school of the Redeemed Christian Church of God is not operational. Some schools have also been planted in many foreign nations.

" When some blessings come the recipient rejoice; when some blessings come the recipient regrets. "

- Enoch Adeboye -

REDEEMER'S UNIVERSITY FOR NATIONS (RUN)

The vision of Redeemer's University of Nations (RUN) had always been like a seed in the heart of Pastor Adeboye. Sickened by the epileptic conditions of the Government University System in Nigeria which had become a breeding ground for cultism, and strike actions which could keep students at home for months and sometimes a whole session, Pastor Adeboye determined to start a University of choice which would promote academic excellence, spiritual values, moral integrity and would not tolerate any cult activities or strike actions.

In 1993, the Federal Government of Nigeria launched the Decree no 9 which created the opportunity for the establishment of Private Universities in Nigeria. Things began to look positive towards the realization of this dream to own a University of renown. Pastor Adeboye set up a 25 man committee of seasoned and distinguished academics and professionals and charged them with the mandate of doing the groundwork towards the establishment of the Redeemer's University of Nations. The team was to report directly to the office of the General Overseer. After much efforts by the committee, in December 2003, the Nigerian University Commission authorized the mission to establish a University on its present temporary site at the Redemption City. To the glory of God, the University opened its doors and took in the first set of students in 2004. Since inception, the University has distinguished itself as a University of high class with State of the Art Facilities and equipments. Presently, there are over 5,000 students. The vision of the University is to promote mental excellence in a conducive atmosphere, to raise a new generation of leaders who would reshape the new Nigeria and the world at large and to model spiritual and moral standards. The University aims to be the best University in the world within the first ten years of its existence.

As part of his commitment to education, in 2001, Pastor Adeboye launched the Education Week within the mission. During this special period, emphasis is placed on education in all the parishes of the RCCG. Different academic competition programmes are held among all the students within the mission. The purpose of the education week is to create awareness in the society on the need for quality education for all young people and to let the students realize that their future is essentially tied to their education.

BIBLE SCHOOL

Pastor Adeboye believes that a sound Christian training facility is one of the major keys to Church growth. RCCG under the directives of Pastor Adeboye has invested heavily in sound Biblical education for the ministers that the mission is producing. The mission has over 40 new training Bible Institutes in different parts of the world.

HABITATION OF HOPE ORPHANAGE

The vision of the Habitation of hope was birthed from the motherly bosom of the wife of Pastor Adeboye and the Mother in Israel of the Redeemed Christian Church of God, Pastor (Mrs.) Foluke Adeboye. She was moved by the suffering of a part of the society which nobody is really looking into; the street boys. She personally gave the assignment to some of the leaders in the Church to evangelise and salvage the street boys who lived at a small village called Kuramo, along the beach in Victoria Island, Lagos and have turned it to a bandits' den. These boys were homeless hoodlums, who lived on the beach under very stringent conditions and dealt in all kinds of hideous things such as selling of Indian hemp, illegal drugs and roadside begging. They were exposed to so many dangers due to the life threatening overflowing nature of the sea. Some of the buildings where these boys took shades and shelter were demolished by the Government, ex- posing them to cold and scorch of the sun. Their lives were really miserable. Many of the boys found themselves on the streets due to the illiteracy, poverty, peer pressure, addiction to illegal drugs, and sometimes malignant neglect by their par- ents or guardians.

" Some blessings can not locate you except you are clothed in the cotton and linen of humility. "

- Enoch Adeboye -

At first, it looked like an impossible mission to reach these boys, a mission impossible due to the wild and outcast life which they had lived and were accustomed to. However, the Lord granted success to the mission and the boys began to respond to the call of salvation and restoration. A number of the boys whom the team of brethren witnessed to received the message of salvation and hope, were fed and clothed and were happy to be returned back to their parents. The boys had come from different parts of Nigeria, such far ends like Zamfara, Cross-River, Oyo, Kaduna and even from the neigh- bouring country of Benin Republic. Those who could not trace their home were taken to the Redemption City where they were rehabilitated. The mission acquired a facility and converted it to Rehabilitation Home where the boys who have been rescued are given a chance to life and education. The story of the Habitation of Hope bears witness to the fact that there is nobody that is so far gone that the saving love of Jesus cannot restore if we are willing to reach out to them.

HERITAGE HOME ORPHANAGE

The Good Women Fellowship, the women arm of the Church following in the steps Pastor Adeboye in 1993 started an orphanage home in response to the cry of countless orphans in the society. Little children are brought to the Heritage Home under different circumstances. Many lost their parents to HIV/AIDS, and due to the dysfunctional state of the society as a result of poverty, many girls take to prostitution to make a living. These girls sometimes have babies and would often abandon them on the streets. Heritage Home is a registered faith based orphanage with over 15 years of positive impact on the society. The home runs with a unique vision to rescue the children from death and give them a chance to have the opportunities of life like education, healthcare, clothing, food, love and support and to be well brought up with Christian values which would enable them to become great leaders of tomorrow. Many children have been adopted into Christian homes where they find the love and support they need.

HOLISTIC OUTREACH

The Holistic Outreach is a very peculiar ministry and is one of the vital Social Service Organs of the RCCG. It reaches out to another neglected part of the Nigerian society; the Prostitutes. The vision was inaugurated on September 28, 2004 and is under the directorate of Pastor (Mrs.) Folu Adeboye, fondly called Mummy G. O. The ministry evangelises Prostitutes within and outside Nigeria. When the girls respond to the ministry, they are taken away from the corrupt environment where they practice prostitution and taken to God's Offspring Home, a rehabilitation home located in Ikorodu, an outskirt of Lagos. As at the time of inauguration, the home had four girls as disciples, one of them was pregnant and it had eight children. Three of the girls were converts from hotels while one was a homeless young single mother.

Prostitution is one of the maladies ravaging the African Continent.

Research has shown that poverty and dysfunctional family system and peer pressure are part of
the major causes of prostitution. Many of the
girls come from extremely poor families and
are subjected to degrading living conditions,
so they opt for prostitution as a means of

" Your blessing is
limited to the extent
of your obedience. "
- Enoch Adeboye -

getting money to feed themselves. Children from polygamous
or broken homes are more prone to embrace prostitution because
they usually lack the love, support and protection of a normal family. Many of these prostitutes are willing to abandon this indecent
lifestyle but there seems to be no other alternative for them. When
the Holistic Outreach ministers the love and saving grace of Christ
to them, they respond in the affirmative. Today many former prostitutes have been rehabilitated, restored and integrated back into the
society as glorious and virtuous women.

There would be no end to writing, if we are to include in this chapter various social services and projects rendered by all the Provinces,
Areas and Parishes of the RCCG both within and outside Nigeria.
In many Nations across the world, the Mission has continued to
benefit its host Nations by contributing in no small measure to its
development and social transformation. Many key world leaders
such as the Mayor of London, the Mayor of New York, the Prince of
Wales, the Governor of Lagos, to mention a few have expressed their
gratitude to Pastor Adeboye because of the laudable social projects
executed by parishes of the Church around the world.

Chapter

18

God's Elder Statesman

The world submitted themselves to king Solomon
not because of his military strength but because of his
spectacular manifold wisdom. This wisdom takes a man
to a position of influence and affluence. It raises a man
to a high status where kings and noble seek his counsel
in the affairs of state governance like Daniel of old.
God's wisdom in the life of Enoch Adeboye, has endeared
him as a counsellor to kings and nobles, a voice for the
needy and afflicted in the society and God's ambassador to
the nations of the world.

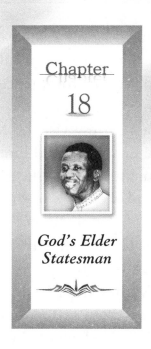

*God's Elder
Statesman*

A nation such as Nigeria with vast ethnic, religious, political and economic diversities and a long history of many conflicts need a unifying voice which commands the attention of all the various interests and Pastor Enoch Adejare Adeboye is that voice. Pastor Adeboye is more than the spiritual head of a Christian denomination; he represents the common interests of all Nigerians and especially the everyday people who do not have someone to speak out in their interest. As a man with long standing reputation of honesty and integrity, he has earned the confidence of the entire Nation. From the political powerhouse in Aso Rock to the ordinary man on the streets, Pastor Adeboye's voice cuts across as God's ambassador for peace, unity and prosperity for the entire Nation.

Amidst the upheavals of Nigeria's political and economic terrain, right from the dark days of military dictatorship to the dawn of democracy in 1999 till present, Pastor Adeboye has continued to lend his voice. He constantly speaks against such societal malignancy like poverty, corruption among public office holders, crime, neglect of basic infrastructures, and abuse of human rights; and always advocate for justice and fairness. Pastor Adeboye is a strong believer in Nigeria and is optimist that Nigeria will ultimately reach her full potentials and have a place of prominence in the community of Nations.

Recently, he was paid a courtesy visit by Mrs. Farida Waziri; Executive Chairman of the Economic and Financial Crimes Commission (EFCC); a government agency. The Executive Chairman led top management staff and members of the board of the anti graft agency to the residence of Pastor Adeboye at Redemption Camp, Lagos – Ibadan Expressway. The General Overseer of the Redeemed Christian Church of God used the opportunity to address the issue of corruption among government officials.

Pastor Adeboye said, "I feel that EFCC is of God. God is behind the reason to establish EFCC". He lamented on the negative effects of corruption on the Nigerian economy. Adeboye said he was shocked by a recent remark that the country would be a paradise if all state governments spend 30 percent of their budget. He said his heart bled when he travelled to Malaysia and saw what the country had done with palm kernel. "They have no oil, no land, no natural resource of any kind but they have good leaders", he said.

> " Many want to issue a simple decree and see it established. But they are not ready to pay the price in their closet. "
> - Enoch Adeboye

Pastor Adeboye said the war against corruption and financial crimes would begin to produce results when the leaders begin to demonstrate the fear of God. He spoke on the ills of compulsive wealth accumulation. He said, "The wealth you acquire through illegal means... you might not live to enjoy it".

He stated how many Nigerian leaders steal from the country's resources and hide them in coded accounts in foreign lands. "Now the money is abroad, they are not there. The money is benefiting the country into which it has been stashed and here we are suffering. And this money is in coded accounts and many of them die suddenly without anybody knowing the code. That money is lost forever."

He enjoined all Nigerians to continue to pray for the EFCC so that the government agency can be effective and not become an instrument of terror.

The EFCC Chairman thanked Pastor Adeboye for sending representation to the launch of the Anti – Corruption Revolution campaign in Abuja last year. She said she had great respect for Pastor Adeboye because of his humility and integrity. She pleaded with him to help mobilize his flock to embrace the fight against corruption and financial crimes.

Due to his position of influence in the society, many politicians always canvass for his endorsements during the elections, but Adeboye gives everybody an equal chance and does not encourage nepotism. Rather, he uses the opportunity to advise the politicians to work towards the greatness of Nigeria if elected into office. He once recalled how two presidential aspirants paid him visits in one day. He joked about how they missed each other by few minutes and wondered what would have happened if they had bumped into each other at his place.

Due to his high level of influence, the Lagos State Government recently requested Pastor Adeboye to do for them a television commercial to encourage the citizens, particularly Christians to pay their taxes, this he gladly accepted. The result of this is that many people who had never considered paying their taxes began to do so because they saw Pastor Enoch Adeboye on TV speaking on the need for them to perform their civil rights as good Christians. A man of great wisdom and deep insights, Pastor Adeboye does not court controversy or violence; he speaks the truth in a way that brings life. In many instances of conflict, the matured manner in which Pastor Adeboye dealt with such matters gave more evidence to the manifold wisdom of God in him.

The issue of poverty in Nigeria is one paramount concern of Pastor Adeboye. He always speaks to the political leaders to do everything within their powers to embark on authentic poverty eradication programs. Recently, he said to the newsmen in Lagos, "I am not an adviser on political issues but a cleric. I know what the people are passing through because I have tasted poverty before" Within his capacity, he has embarked upon many programs such as feeding the poor, providing employment opportunities for the youths and welfare initiatives for the orphans, widows and the elderly to tackle the problem of poverty. Daddy G. O. (General Overseer) as fondly called, always stress on the need for the Nation to acknowledge God and for everyone to conduct their affairs in the fear of the Lord; this he said, would bring peace and prosperity to the Nation. "God does not inflict poverty on people, poverty comes when men oppress one another because of greed," Adeboye once said. One of his popular messages to the Nation through many press interviews is that: "Only God can solve the numerous problems of Nigeria".

In 2000, Adeboye had publicly declared that "Nigeria shall be to the Christians what Mecca is to the Moslems" He went further to affirm that the annual Holy Ghost Congress would be a global event which would draw the whole world to come and worship God in Nigeria and to receive the miracles of the Lord. Nine years later, that prophecy has found its true fulfilment as the Congress has become an annual pilgrimage of a sort, bringing tens of thousands of devotees from all the Continents of the world.

Enoch Adeboye believes strongly in the power of education to liberate the Nation from poverty. He always emphasize on the need for the Nation to focus more on the education sector. He once said in an interview, "Next to salvation (I mean salvation of your soul and everything that goes with it-baptism, the Holy Spirit, etc.) what everybody should have is education. I don't know where I would be today if God did not allow me to be educated." Under his leadership, the Redeemed Christian Church of God (RCCG), has taken up the social responsibility of providing sound education to the people. The Church, has nursery, primary and secondary schools, and also has a college of technology and a University. Altogether, the RCCG has over sixty schools.

Heads of Governments, Heads of States, Governors, Senators, Traditional Kings and many eminent personalities have visited the monthly and annual Holy Ghost Service and Holy Ghost Congress respectively. Pastor Adeboye usually releases words of prophecies to Nigeria and to the Nations of the world in December of each year.

> " Church or ministerial activities can never replace a thriving relationship with Christ. Ministers are in hell because they sought activities, not relationship. "
> - Enoch Adeboye -

Those words of prophecies always come to pass; not one word of God through his anointed servant has gone unfulfilled.

One of the Former Presidents of the Federal Republic of Nigeria, commenting on God's servant Pastor Adeboye said, "Pastor Adeboye is a most humble man who goes about the propagation of the gospel with utmost simplicity and under the inspiration of the Holy Spirit. I often feel overwhelmed by the way he walks in the revelation of God in man. The way he delivers the revelation from the throne of grace makes God Almighty (through the Holy Spirit) so practical and real in his ministry. Having encountered God the way I did, being at meetings with Pastor Adeboye redoubles the presence of the Holy Spirit of God in such refreshing measure that keeps my faith and confidence resolute and strong. Most touching is the dramatically real manner in which Pastor Adeboye switches from one level of revelation to another. His capacity to receive from the throne of mercy is humbling in its force of authority, making charisma and simplicity to be too captivating for me to resist". Pastor Adeboye carries the presence of the Holy Spirit so distinctly that it cannot be mistaken. One can therefore not but be inspired by a man with such supernatural endowment. It is simply humbling and reassuring that, with living testimonies like Pastor Adeboye of the mysteries of God's essence and divinity, which confirms the immutability of God's oath and promise, I have daily reassurance that the God that called me will see me through the challenge of rebuilding Nigeria's democratic foundation.

"As I am daily reassured that God gave us the likes of Pastor Adeboye, like the old prophets, as a mark of love for a country and a world for which he has a purpose, as instruments of God for showering blessings and greatness on Nigeria, it is a fearful thing to toy with the destiny of a country that the Almighty delights in.

Pastor Adeboye is thoroughly distinguished, not by his activities, but by the grace of the Lord upon his life. If God should raise up men who, while they are still here, could share in their burden and, after them, could keep the torch of the supernatural ever aglow, Enoch Adeboye stands shoulder high".

He also creates time to serve the interest of other Churches. For many years, Pastor Adeboye served as the President of the Pentecostal Fellowship of Nigeria.

Chapter

19

*Global
Impact*

There is a key that opens the gates to the nations of the world. When God said, I will give unto you the nations of the earth for your inheritance and the uttermost parts of the world for your possession, he meant to deliver to his chosen ones this master keys which unlocks the nations from all races, tribes, colours and tongues. It is God's will and purpose that the whole world would be reached with the Gospel before the Second Coming of Christ, therefore Enoch Adeboye does not see the white nor the black, he does not see also the rich or poor, male or female, God has given him the eyes that only sees souls dying to be saved.

Chapter
19

*Global
Impact*

The continent of Africa is presently at the prime of one of the greatest revival movements in the history of Christianity. The demography of the Church has shifted from its old heartlands in Europe and America and found a resting place in Africa. The Church in Africa is experiencing growth at unprecedented dimensions. In the midst of the depressingly predictable news and images from which we create our perceptive of the Continent is the emergence of its rapidly increasing Christian Churches and denominations that serve as oases of integrity and heralds of hope; the very exact opposite of all that is seemingly wrong with Africa.

The prophecy of Isaiah has found its fulfilment amongst the Christians in Africa. "The people that walked in darkness have seen a great light: they that dwell in the land of the shadow of death, upon them hath the light shined". At the centre of the great movement of the Spirit of God on the Continent of Africa is the powerful and penetrating force of the Gospel through the Redeemed Christian Church of God under the leadership of Pastor E. A. Adeboye.

When Martin Luther the reformer was excommunicated from the

Roman Catholic Church, he made a bold assertion; "the world is my chapel." It seems that Adeboye shares the same conviction. In October 2000, in Jerusalem Israel, he introduced himself saying, "I am Brother Enoch Adeboye, Made in heaven, Assembled in Nigeria and Exported to the world". The man Adeboye sees the whole world as a single empire to conquer for Jesus Christ. Language, racism, finances, strict visa regulations, the list of barriers is endless but Adeboye does not seem to see any of them. Like Alexander the Great he marches onward to conquer the whole world, but for Christ and not with the edge of the sword but with the life-giving weapon of the Word of God and violent prayers. J. Grant Swank, Jr., a South African writer on contemporary Christian theology has noted "This is the face of 21st-Century Christianity: Big, Restless and African. There is no better symbol of it than the Redeemed Church and the insatiable ambitions of its guiding hand and Pastor, Rev. Enoch Adejare Adeboye. (He) leads the fastest-growing Christian movement from a continent that is rapidly putting its stamp on the faith around the world."

" If for any reason you use your tongue to wipe your plate, you have no iota of self control. Eat with a knife at your throat always! "
- Enoch Adeboye -

He also said, "Many theologians say the 'African century' of Christianity is under way." If so, then populous and English-speaking Nigeria is its spiritual homeland, and Churches like Pastor Adeboye's are its vanguard. Its driven leadership, loose global oversight and staggering cash flow make up precisely the formula that so alarm many traditional denominations. "What began as a living-room Bible study in 1952 is now a juggernaut ~ a University, movie studio, satellite television and a Wi-Fi Internet provider. Now add to that millions of followers in more than 90 nations, including footholds in China and even Dallas".

At geometric growth rate of almost 300 percent annually, the Redeemed Christian Church of God under the leadership of Pastor Adeboye continues to expand to the nooks and corners of the world. The Church boasts of over 20,000 networks of Churches which is referred to as parishes in Nigeria alone with membership of over 5 million. Presently, the Church is represented in 110 Nations of the world and claims to have close to 500,000 converts in all these Nations. The unimaginable dimension of such growth suggests that such feat can only be accomplished by the Almighty God through vessels that are empowered by the Holy Spirit.

Pastor Adeboye the humble leader who is pioneer of this great revival movement is not yet satisfied. He still has greater visions to spread the word of God to every single person in the world and for the Church to experience more growth. He said his vision is to have a member of the Redeemed Christian Church of God in every family in the world; to plant a parish of the Church within every five minutes driving distance of developed nations and within every five minutes walking distance of developing nations. Can this vision become a reality? The track records speak for it. If the Church had grown from forty parishes to over 20,000 parishes in less than three decades, then it would be a matter of time before they accomplish this lofty vision.

The Allied Press in the United States of America have also noted the massive work and growth of the Redeemed Christian Church of God. Rachel Zoll, AP Religion writer commented on the strategic approach of the Church at winning souls and planting Churches in the United States of America. She wrote, "On the 25th floor of a luxury office tower, a Church most people have never heard of is planning to save America. The Redeemed Christian Church of God was founded in Lagos by men and women who were once the target of missionary work themselves. Now their Church is one of the most aggressive evangelists to emerge from the recent advance of Christianity across Africa, and their offices in the high-tech corridor of greater Dallas reflect the group's bold, entrepreneurial approach.

She further attest, "Over the last century, Christians in the West African nation have swelled from a tiny minority to nearly half the population, and its Pastors have shown an exceptional talent for winning new believers abroad. In the United States, the Redeemed Church is ahead of them all. The Church has opened more than 200 parishes in just over a decade, from Chicago and Atlanta to Washington and New York, and is training Americans of all races to help them reach beyond the African immigrant community. One of their largest congregations, Victory Temple in Bowie, MD, claims 2,000 members".

The Redeemed Christian Church of God is presently on the frontline and growing at a rate which baffles the mainstream American Churches. Recently, the Church acquired more than 600 acres of farm land which is located about fifty miles north of Dallas. On the land, the Church is building a multimillion-dollar National Headquarters and Conference Complex in rural Floyd, Texas. Also, the RCCG in America under the flagship of Dove Media has launched a satellite television which broadcasts the teachings of Daddy G. O. and other anointed servants of the Lord. As part of the efforts to reach the entire United States with the Gospel, an internet radio station is also broadcasting 24hours of the day. The Church opened the first parish in the U.S.A in 1992, when Pastor Enoch Adeboye prayed in a Detroit living room with a Nigerian engineer who was working for Ford. Today, there are parishes of the Church in almost all the States in America and the Annual Holy Ghost Service in Madison Square Garden in New York attracts thousands of worshippers. The RCCG in Canada is also experiencing tremendous growth.

In Europe, the Church has gained much ground and experienced tremendous growth. There are branches of the Church in Belgium, Bulgaria, Denmark, France, Germany, Greece, Ireland, Norway, Portugal, Romania, Scotland, Spain, Sweden, and Switzerland. In the

United Kingdom, the Church has experienced drastic growth. It is hard to give a definite statistics of the growth of the Church because new parishes are emerging on daily basis. However, as at early 2008, there are 276 parishes in London, North England has 60 parishes, and Scotland has 16 parishes bringing the total number to 352 parishes of the Redeemed Christian Church of God in the UK alone. In 2008, Christianity Today rated the Redeemed Christian Church of God as the fastest growing Church in London and Europe. The UK version of the Holy Ghost Service called Festival of Life is the largest gathering of Christians in Europe with over 60,000 people in attendance. The meeting has been graced by political figures in the UK such as the Mayor of London.

In 2007, Prince Charles, Prince of Wales celebrated his birthday in company of his wife Lady Camilla, Duchess of Cornwall at Jesus House, a parish of the Redeemed Christian Church of God. The service was attended by eminent personalities from the Royal family and top clergy in England. Prince Charles who was excited at the love and honour which the people showered on him said, "I can't tell you what a joy it is to worship with you today. All I can tell you is that there is nowhere else I would rather be on my birthday". He also commented on the positive impact which the Redeemed Christian Church of God is making in the UK as a society, "In your Church, you are doing the things that Jesus would do if He walked the streets of London today. You are all a marvellous example of how so many people whose family originate from the Commonwealth have brought new life into the Christian Church in the United Kingdom thereby completing the cycle started by missionaries from Britain so many years ago. So we have that to thank you for". On a final note, Prince Charles spoke on possible collaboration

> " Obedience to heavenly laws compels obedience from earthly subjects and activities. "
>
> - Enoch Adeboye -

between the Redeemed Christian Church of God and his charity initiative, The Prince's Trust.

The Church also has many branches in Australia, Russia, China, Bahamas, Fiji Islands, Japan, Hong Kong, Haiti, United Arab Emirates and many other nations where the Gospel of Jesus Christ has not yet been saturated. Everywhere the Church went; it takes along two strategies to reach the people. The first is the preaching of the Gospel and the second is community service. To the glory of God, many schools, hospitals, feeding projects, and community projects have been carried out by thousands of parishes of the RCCG all over the world. For an example, after the end of the long war in Liberia, Pastor Enoch Adeboye was one of the leaders to respond as part of the rebuilding process in the Nation. An envoy was sent to the nation with relief materials. The Church has since been part of the nation rebuilding in that country by embarking on various projects including the construction of schools for the young people.

" Satan did not create the sun so he cannot stop it. Satan did not create you so he cannot stop you. "
- Enoch Adeboye

Chapter

20

Awards & Honours
The World's
49th Most
Influential Person

Goodness and mercy, honour and dignity, riches and wealth, favour and grace are companions of those who walk in the footsteps of Jesus. When you choose to serve the Lord in truth and in spirit, the world will serve your interest and promote your cause. Despite his unwillingness to court the praise of men, Pastor Adeboye continually finds his path being trailed by these amiable companions listed above. When the heavens open upon a man's life and God's voice of endorsement speak out in his favour, the world will hear him, multitudes will follow him and his voice will echo to the corners of the world. This is the testimony of Pastor Enoch Adeboye and it can be yours too if you choose to walk in the same footsteps of Jesus.

Chapter

20

Awards & Honours
The World's
49th Most
Influential Person

THE IMAGE IN THE SAND

Pastor Enoch Adejare Adeboye is a man who does not love the praise of men. He prefers to dwell in the secret place of the Most High and abide under the shadow of the Almighty. Early in his ministry, the Lord had taught him a timeless lesson on humility. Once, the Lord asked him to go to the seaside. When he got there, the Lord instructed him to draw the image of a man in the sand and to use his feet to wipe it out. At that point, the Lord gave him one of the most important instructions of his life, He said, "the day you entertain the praise of men, I would wipe you out like the image in the sand." Since then, Pastor Adeboye has intentionally kept a low personal profile. He wraps himself up in the humility of Christ. No matter how loud the world sings his praises, he would never assume the glory to himself, but return all the glory to God. The amazing thing about serving the Lord in humility is that just as the Bible says, the more one humbles himself under the Mighty Hand of the Lord the higher the Lord exalts his anointed servants. In as much as Pastor Adeboye runs away from being seen, without seeking for it, without realizing it, the majestic honour of the Lord continues to follow him everywhere he goes. Many nations and organizations of repute around the world have bestowed different honours and awards on Pastor Adeboye but he does not take them into much account or make reference to them in his sermons.

THE GLOBAL ELITE

Then along came one big honour, which Pastor Adeboye did not even have the chance to either accept or refuse. It was not the kind of honour that could be couriered to your private box and kept in the shelf neither was it the kind that you could send a representative to receive. This time, there is no hiding place for the gold fish; NEWSWEEK, the renowned and prestigious international magazine in the United States had carried out a survey of the world's 50 most influential personalities in the year 2008/2009, which the magazine referred to as The Global Elite and Pastor E.A. Adeboye fits on the list as the 49th most influential personality in the world. The news which hit the world by storm was released in a classic report published by Newsweek on December 20, 2008 with the caption; "A Pentecostal preacher from Nigeria has made big plans to save your soul". In our world which is almost overtaken by secularism and humanism, Adeboye standing tall among the global elites, has drawn the attention of the world to God, Christianity and the Pentecostal movement.

The visionary and flawless leadership of Pastor Adeboye's long years in ministry as the General Overseer of the Redeemed Christian Church of God bears witness to this global recognition. Pastor Adeboye goes about his assignment of sharing the good Word of the Lord quietly and the outcome of the work is proclaimed to the whole world. Just as the holy writ says, "who can light a candle and put it in a secret place?" In what seemed like a prophetic word, Adeboye declared to newsmen in an interview in October 2005, "I have been doing my own thing quietly and I believe that sooner or later it would yield results". Being the only African listed with three other Blacks and the only Christian Clergy, the recognition is not just for Adeboye as a person, or the RCCG as a Church entity, it is recognition for all African people and essentially for the Body of Christ all over the world.

From an impoverished background in tiny Ifewara, Enoch Adeboye committed himself to discipline and hard work which made him first among equals when he bagged a Ph.D in Applied Mathematics and became a University professor at the young age of 30. In his quest for deeper meaning to life, he encountered Jesus Christ and the Lord revealed to him the original purpose of his being; to become God's spokesman to the nations of the world. Like Moses of old, Adeboye suffered many tribulations at the back of the desert of life but he did not waiver in his faith. He abandoned his prestigious career as a senior lecturer at the University of Ilorin in 1981 to become the General Overseer of the Redeemed Christian Church of God. After three decades of vigorous service and commitment to the Lord's work, the RCCG under the leadership of Adeboye has grown as a tiny mustard seed from just 39 branches to over 20,000 branches in 110 countries. God has proven Adeboye's work such that the prestigious NEWSWEEK refer to him as "one of the most successful preachers in the world." A man who has held on to integrity and uprightness, the NEWSWEEK acknowledged these virtues in Adeboye. "While other Pentecostal Pastors have been accused of financial misdeeds or faking supernatural powers, Adeboye remains above the fray, and Nigerian government and leaders seek his input on pressing social issues," the magazine further affirmed.

Who would have thought that Enoch Adejare Adeboye the son of a poor farmer from the tiny village of Ifewara would later in life be listed among the movers and shakers of the world? The life and ministry of Adeboye bears witness to the faithfulness of God towards those who serve him in spirit and in truth and that it pays to live a life of humility, discipline and hard work which are not easy to come by in our modern times. Adeboye, a big dreamer who serves a God of miracles has not given up on his quest to win the world for Christ. According to the NEWSWEEK magazine, "He wants to save souls, and he wants to do so by planting Churches the way Starbucks used to build coffee shops: everywhere". Speaking of his immediate future plans, he told NEWSWEEK, "In the developing world we say we want Churches to be within five minutes' walk of every person, in the developed world, we say five minutes of driving." As lofty as these visions seem, they would come to pass because Adeboye serves a God Who confirms the word of his servant, and performs the counsel of his messengers.

NIGERIA'S LIVING LEGENDS AWARD & NATIONAL MERIT AWARD

Whilst the millions of spiritual children of Daddy G.O as Pastor Adeboye is fondly called all across the world were still caught up in a glorious euphoria concerning the NEWSWEEK recognition, more honours continued to roll out in succession in recognition of the work of the Lord. On Tuesday, June 16, Pastor Adeboye clinched the maiden edition of Nigeria's Greatest Living Legends contest initiated by the Vanguard Media Limited and Silverbird Group a National TV in Nigeria to celebrate great achievements by illustrious Nigerians in their various fields of human endeavour. The honour was the climax of the collation of votes cast by Nigerians through text messages in which Adeboye scored 30.8 per cent to top the list of 20 nominees, with four runners-up. Still speaking of awards and honours, Adeboye God's man, was one of the few Nigerians with different National Awards which is the epitome of civil recognition in Nigeria. Pastor Enoch Adeboye was conferred with the honour of Commander of the Order of Niger (OON). In response to all the honours, Adeboye did not take it for himself, but gave it back to those he said the honours belonged to, the RCCG family. Pastor Adeboye told members of his Church that he did not accept all the honours and awards for his person but for them. He said, "It not me they are honouring, it is you, your Church."

Chapter
21

This Is Just
The Beginning

The fulfilment of God's vision does not have an end;
it graduates and finds its expression from one level of
glory to another. When the early Church thought that
Paul had reached the climax of his ministry, he refuted
the idea and told them, 'I forget the things that are past and
I press forward.' When at the age of eighty, Caleb should
have been planning for his retirement; he was seeing
visions of more conquests and demanding for his right to
the mountains. With record breaking ministry feats,
one would expect Daddy G.O as fondly called, to have
reached the utmost height yet he goes to the top of
the mountains and sees more grounds to be conquered
for Christ. He continuously tells the Church, 'what we
have done is nothing compared to what is yet to be done'.
He has the outlandish vision to plant a Church in every
fifteen minutes walking distance in developing countries
and five minutes driving distance in developed countries.
He also dares to dream of planting a Redeemed
Christian Church of God member in every household of
the world. There is no retirement in the army of God.

Chapter
21

This Is
Just The
Beginning

"On the shores of hesitation lies the bones of countless millions who at the dawn of success waited and while waiting died."

Robert Schuller

For Pastor Enoch Adeboye and the Redeemed Christian Church of God, the best is yet to come. Inspired by the same vision to evangelise the whole world that gave him a head start at the beginning, Adeboye is still marching forward on his quest to take the world for Jesus. He constantly challenges the entire RCCG family not to be satisfied with the victory of yesterday and the glory of today but to press forward towards the possibilities of tomorrow. He assures them that the Church has not yet reached its fullest potentials and that greater days still lay ahead. In a recent interview, Pastor Adeboye poured out his heart on the future and role the Church would play in it, "The way forward as we have often said is that the Church must realise that it has not yet arrived. We shouldn't believe that the Church has become so big a giant. Yes, we are growing no doubt but there is yet much ground to cover" Adeboye is not alone in this holy fervour never to be satisfied but to yearn for more. Paul a

First Century Church Apostle wrote to the Ephesian Church, "My brothers, I do not count myself to have taken possession, but one thing I do, forgetting the things behind and reaching forward to the things before. I press toward the mark for the prize of the high calling of God in Christ Jesus". Phil. 3:13-14.

Adeboye acknowledges God as the mighty Performer of all the mighty works going on in the Redeemed Christian Church of God and he enjoins every member of the Church to keep their hearts stayed on Him. "If you think about the fact that we are where we are today by the grace of God and by the prayers of yesteryears, then we have to realise that if we have to get to where we are going, we have to pray more" Obviously, Pastor Adeboye is not carried away by the euphoria of the success of the RCCG and its global impact. Like the patriarchs of old, he keeps a straight head, a burdened heart and set his eyes on posterity. He said, "Again, we need to appreciate the fact that because the Almighty God has blessed us, prospered us and increased us, we need to realise that to whom much is given, much is required. In other words, we need to tighten our belts and be ready to move forward".

> " Several Christian families are empowering Satan to take hold of their homes by making the family altar (devotion) a rarity. "
>
> - Enoch Adeboye -

Another amazing thing is that Adeboye's passion and zeal for the Kingdom has increased immensely. He goes about his assignment with a holy fervour and tight schedule which is not usual for someone of his age. At 67, Pastor Adeboye has the energy of a youth. He is physically agile and still dreaming big dreams; he is particularly blessed with very good sight. He works round the clock and does not have one second to spare to idleness. A man who has discipline and hard work for watchword made it clear that the standard of discipline in the Church is not going to change. "We must of course also appreciate the fact that the Church is an army of God and the only way to destroy an army is to introduce indiscipline into its midst. We must realize that this army is going to be razor sharp for the Almighty God; we are going to remain at the cutting edge of visions and activities for the Almighty God and therefore discipline is forever going to be the order of the day"

In the arena of strategic evangelism Adeboye is an authority. He has successfully shifted the Church from a small denomination with only 39 branches to the global phenomenon that it is today. It would therefore not be empty words or wishful thinking, when he lays out his plans for the future. Charging the Church to be repositioned for greater harvest, he revealed the strategy that would help the Church to fulfil her greater destiny. "So the way forward is to pray, evangelise and remain as the cutting-edge of the Almighty God.

If a child's first pet were an elephant, one wonders what he would have for a pet when he finally grows up, maybe a dinosaur.

Final Word : Destiny Is Calling You Too

The world is yet to fully experience what God can do through yielded vessels that are empowered by His Spirit. Among the multitudes of baby Christians, there is emerging a remnant of mighty men and women of valour. God is raising a new breed without greed. This remnant army stands ready to reclaim their spiritual authority and walk in a divine dominion that will eclipse everything we've known in a by-gone millennium. A people so strong and mighty, they will adamantly oppose all human standards and set new records in every area of human endeavour. This end-time remnant generation of overcomers constitutes a people who do not stumble in the face of opposition nor crumble in the face of criticism and intimidation. In fact they are actually engaged in the arena of conflict.

An army of a people who love nothing but God, and hate nothing but sin, a people whose passion is to win souls for God at all costs. They count their lives as a price to pay to attain to the fulfilment of a great cause. They are ready at all times to sacrifice and be sacrificed for the cause of Christ. These are a people whose bodies bear the scars of a valiant soldier, whose souls attest to the advancing armies of their alien enemies but whose spirits know the aspiration of soaring to great heights. Their spirits understand something that the ordinary mind cannot comprehend, something that is tagged impossible by the norms of the day. In the strength of the Lord, they scale the utmost heights. They understand the grandeur and splendour of fresh discoveries and enjoy the thrills of fighting for a righteous cause.

Men and women who are possessed by the anointing of the Holy Ghost operate in the realm of fire, so no earthly fire can consume them. They use the supernatural force of God to influence the destinies of nations and great cities. These are men and women who turn the world upside down. Huge crowds gather to listen to their words and great professors of this world bow their knees at the revelation of heaven's wisdom through unlearned men. They are inspired by words like; impossible, insurmountable, insufferable, and incurable. It is not an army of the majority, but just like Gideon's army, it's just a band of men from among the multitudes.

If you would come before the Holy One, on mount Zion together where there is innumerable company of angels, the glory of the Lord would be revealed to you. You will experience transformation from the realm of the natural to the supernatural. You will behold the awesome presence of the King of glory; humbly, you will bow your knees in worship with hands lifted up in reverence of the Mighty One and songs of praises will become the fruits of your lips.

Yes, the Sun of righteousness doth arise with healing in His wings, set to heal, deliver and to save. These are the days to see the deaf hear, the blind see, the lame walk, the dead raised back to life, burdens lifted, broken homes and marriages restored. The barren is set free, lives are transformed, unbelievers are drawn to Christ, the backslidden return to the God of salvation, youths are renewed in strength and vigour; destinies are remoulded, making shouts of joy and victory the order of the day. A definite encounter with the glory of Jesus Christ comes with great power; a power so strong, that it makes the impossible, possible. Just one encounter of this glory can change your life forever.

Don't stay any longer by the pool of Bethesda, waiting for somebody to push you in. Stop waiting on God to act when in actual sense, God is waiting for you to act. It is time for you to take a plunge into the living springs. Get plugged to the source of the power and see yourself becoming the person you never thought you could be, and go places you thought were unreachable. Do not petition the courts of heaven for assignments equal to your natural powers; rather plead upon your knees for Holy Ghost power that is equal to your assignments. You can also be a part of this great army. You can get possessed by the Spirit of breakthroughs and take your prophetic position in God's End-Time Army. This is God's day. This is God's hour. Now is the hour when God will dispatch His men full of authority to exercise absolute power and dominion. The question is, Will you join God's end-time army? Destiny is calling you too!

Acknowledgements

In a cave in the Islamic Republic of Iran, I'm stuck with the task of attempting to list those that have made the dream of writing this masterpiece a reality. Looking round at my environment, in the midst of people eagerly seeking the truth and freedom in a place which directly contends with the accomplishment of this dream, I have come to appreciate first and foremost the liberty I have received through the saving power of Jesus Christ.

Without much ado, I say a wonderful thank you to the love of my life, my mentor, life coach, friend and partner, Rev Bible Davids. Sweetie, you definitely have been that instrument in God's hand used to propel me to do more and be all I can be. Your resolute poise and vigour are the secret ingredients that keep me going.

A million hugs goes to the world's best Dad and Mum, Rev Drs' Ed and Charlotte Edwards who tutored me from birth. You both taught me my first words of prayers and the scriptures. Your countless supports, sacrifices, care and confidence cannot be ignored. I couldn't have had it better.

These pages cannot capture the numerous people that have made this work a possibility. My heart goes out to Mummy G. O. Pastor Foluke Adeboye, Pastor Tokunbo Olorunimbe, Leke Adeboye, Doyin, Pastors' Godwin and Liz Smith, Rev & Mrs Mike Edwards, Rev John Oluwasanmi, Pastors' Sola and Taiwo Odubiyi's, Pastors' Tunde and Ola Ewedemi, Pastors' Ladi and Taiwo Thompson, Henry and Erica Obike, Mary, Samuel, Emmanuel and every other person I have not mentioned. Thanks a million.

Finally to all those I have not mentioned, you are highly appreciated.

275

Select Bibliography and Picture Credits

Bola Olawale, *Gem Woman, Inspiring Women to Aspire*, July/August 2008

Dr Olusola Ajayi, *Warriors of Righteousness (The Life and Ministry of Rev J. O. Akindayomi)*, Ordinance Printing House

E. A Adeboye, *Time of Favour*, RCCG Region 10 (Abuja Family) 2009

E. A. Adeboye, *Marriage that brings down God's Glory (Guidelines for Youths and Adults)*, CRM Bookshops

Folahan Nwabuogo Adefope, *For Such a Time As This, A Portrait of Foluke Adeboye*, Kingdom Link House, June 2008

Folake Adeniyi, *Folu Adeboye: A Labourer in His Vineyard*, Bostar Publishing Ltd, 2006

Olanike Olaleru in collaboration with Collins Egbo, *The seed in the Ground (The story of the founding of The Redeemed Christian Church of God)* Father of Light Publishers

Olusegun Olu Olusanya, *Redeemer's International Magazine*, Issue 1, 2006

Pastor E. A Adeboye, *Sermons of the 2001 Holy Ghost Services*, 2002

Pastor E. A Adeboye, *(Sermons tapes)* 2009, 2008, 2007, 2006, 2005, 2004, 2003, 2000, 1999

Pastor E. A. Adeboye, *E-Open Heavens, Compendium Series*, 2009, 2008, 2007, 2006

Pastor E. A. Adeboye, *Open Heavens*, Volume Eight, 2008

RCCG, *Redemption Light, A monthly Publication of The Redeemed Christian Church of God*, December 2008

RCCG, *Redemption Light, A monthly Publication of The Redeemed Christian Church of God*, March 2009

RCCG, *Redemption Light, A monthly Publication of The Redeemed Christian Church of God*, May 2009

RCCG, *Redemption Testimonies*, CRM Press 2008

RCCG, *Walking with God, The Testimony of The Redeemed Christian Church of God Redeemed at 50*

Tony Ojo, *Let somebody shout Halleluyah*, Honeycombs Cards and Prints

VCD *The Covenant Church*, Dove Media, 2006

www.christiantoday.com   www.allafrica.com

www.go.sturvs.com   www.odili.net

www.prayersfire.com   www.assatashakur.org

www.mask.org.za   www.newsweek.com

Picture Credits

Debo

Farid A. Ghori & Jons Arun Michel - Graphic Inlay

Index